PRAISE FOR THE AUTHORS AND *IN F*

Ilchi Lee's transcendent work is a constant inspiration, and I am deeply pleased to witness the increasing worldwide influence of Brain Education.

—**Oscar Arias Sanchez**, Nobel Peace Laureate

Ilchi Lee and Jessie Jones have skillfully combined knowledge from a variety of complementary and alternative domains to provide a highly readable and thought-provoking manual that links physical and mental activities into a holistic program designed to promote successful aging. Combining wisdom found in Western and Eastern philosophies, Lee and Jones provide practical and easy-to-implement strategies that will help promote physical and mental health and well-being.

—**Wojtek Chodzko–Zajko, Ph.D.**, president, International Society for Aging and Physical Activity

To age gracefully is not easy. We need all the help we can get. *In Full Bloom* is that one-of-a-kind help. It is an East-West synthesis of both knowledge and wisdom that idle-age and senior adults will find enlightening and practically helpful. A must-read for people who want to live their later years, not only gracefully, but also with life and vitality.

—**Norman Lawson SPM, Ph.D.**, clinical psychologist

In Full Bloom offers simple, yet profound steps to help you fully realize your potential. Every phase of life should be engaging and invigorating. This easy to read guide shows you the way.

—**David Bishop**, president, Sony Pictures Home Entertainment

This book does a big favor for those of us who know we are aging! The philosophy and approach presented respects our aging brain, and in a comfortable, easy-to-read style tells us on how our brains should continue to work for us and make us perform at our best. The East and West influence of the exercises presented makes this approach special. I have personally practiced almost all the exercises described here and found many of them fun. These exercises speak to us and tell us that the sky is the limit! They have truly fostered my intuitive side. What could be more rewarding?

    —**Mariam R. Chacko**, M.D., Baylor College of Medicine, Houston, TX

Everyone is to age and then die. If one can live with full health in body and mind right until death, the burden from fear of death may be much lighter. This wonderful book will give people a better chance to realize this hope.

    —**Hee-Sup Shin**, National Scientist Awardee of Korea

Ilchi Lee offers a common sense way to fulfillment for every individual. His philosophy guides us to a peaceful world in which all living creatures are accorded respect and compassionate treatment.

    —**Seymour Topping**, author and professor of journalism

This book is the proof we've been looking for that "old dogs CAN learn new tricks"…and even create new ones which will challenge the young. By integrating Western processes and Eastern practices, one will discover a fountain of health, happiness and peace. Apply the five BEST options shared by Ilchi Lee and Jessie Jones, and live your BEST life yet as you become the CEO of your mind!

    —**Birgit D. Kamps**, CEO, HireSynergy

IN FULL BLOOM

A BRAIN EDUCATION GUIDE
FOR
SUCCESSFUL AGING

ILCHI LEE AND JESSIE JONES, PH.D.

BEST Life Media
6560 Highway 179, Ste.114
Sedona, AZ 86351
www.bestlifemedia.com
1-877-504-1106

This book should be regarded as a reference source and is not intended
to replace professional medical advice. Seek the advice of your physician
before beginning this or any other fitness program. The authors and the
publishers disclaim any liability arising directly or indirectly from the
use of this book.

First paperback edition: 2008
Library of Congress Control Number: 2008920809

If you are unable to purchase this book from your local book seller, you
can order through www.bestlifemedia.com or www.amazon.com,
or by calling 1-877-504-1106.

Wrinkles should merely indicate where smiles have been.
—Mark Twain

Contents

Chapter 5: Your Masterful Brain 153

Brain Mastering Activities 165

Afterword: Embodying the Jangsaeng Ideal 173

Appendix

ACKNOWLEDGMENTS

Special thanks to Tim Vandehey and Nicole Dean for bringing just the right style and tone to the writing of this book; to Jiyoung Oh for her guidance in bringing this book to fruition at BEST Life Media; to Nora Lee and Jason Cessna for the development of the Brain Education for Successful Aging program; to Yoori Kim and Ji-in Kim for bringing the design of this book to full blossom; to Al Choi for his charming sketches; to Edward Randolph, Gaye Anthony, Karon Miller, and Mary Dunton for striking the perfect poses; to Tara Kim and the Dahn Foundation for their dedication to bringing Brain Education to seniors; and to the many healers and practitioners whose dedication and enthusiasm bring so much to so many through Brain Education.

INTRODUCTION

Healthy Brain, Healthy Aging

The brain is the seat of our humanity. The first spark of brainwave activity marks the beginning of each human life; the final cessation of that activity marks that life's end. Every experience, emotion, and memory reaches us through the brain's mediation. It is the source of all our art, science, and culture. Powered by untold trillions of neural connections, we hug our children, learn to hit a baseball, write first novels, pray to our gods, and reach out to help our fellows in need. In practical terms, we are our brains.

Consequently, it can be disturbing to reach middle age or beyond and hear what the popular media has to say about the things that are in store for our brains as we grow older. Our culture is filled with images of aged individuals whose minds are foggy, confused, and useless. When we think of old age and the brain, we think of words such as *dementia, Alzheimer's disease,* and *Parkinson's disease.* Even if our thoughts are not concerned with such doom and gloom, conventional wisdom still tells us that finding a vigorous, creative, energetic, improving brain in an aging body is as rare as finding buried treasure at the bottom of the ocean.

None of us like to think about losing our memory or our ability to think and reason as we age. Yet that is precisely what most of us believe will happen no matter what we do. So we passively accept the notion of becoming forgetful and assume it's inevitable. We fret over memory lapses in our fifties and sixties and worry that we are experiencing an early onset of Alzheimer's or some other form of dementia. We tell uneasy jokes about seniors who have lost their identities and laugh while we pray that we won't be the butt of someone else's joke when we're ninety. Well, perhaps it's high time for some myth-busting about the aging brain.

The Truth About Age and the Brain

For more than twenty-five years, we have worked to understand the truth about the brain and its role as the source and mediator of all human activity. More importantly, we have sought knowledge about the ways that each of us can tap the brain's virtually limitless potential for growth, happiness, and peaceful, healthful living. In our search, we have discovered a new truth about the brain: It is infinitely adaptable. Because our brains are the final determinants of our culture, consciousness, and behavior, by developing our brains as we would develop a muscle, we give ourselves the power to change our reality. Our brains make our world; it is high time we took control of our brains to make a world we want to live in.

In this book, we will show you that instead of passively accepting outdated ideas of the aging brain, you can take an active role in helping your brain evolve and unleash its potential. Brain Education System Training (BEST) is a method through which you can develop your innate human capacities for health, well-being, achievement, and inner peace through optimal management of your brain. With BEST, you can teach your brain to become more productive and creative even as you age. You can foster greater harmony between your mind and your body and discover new joy and peace in your life and in the world around you. In essence, you can defy traditional thinking about the aging brain and enjoy more mental agility and enhanced creativity in later life.

The information presented in this book is neither guesswork nor wishful thinking. It is the result of years of scientific and experiential study of the brain's nature and its responsiveness to the actions of the body. It is also the product of Ilchi Lee's work with yoga, health and wellness education, meditation, and other Asian traditions that unify mind and body into a healthful, integrated whole, as well as Dr. Jessie Jones's work, especially in gerokinesiology, the specialized science of the ways in which exercise and aging interact.

The truth about the aging brain is simple but extraordinary: Although some loss of clarity and memory skill is inevitable as the years go by, much of the brain's aging process is within your control. You can have a fit brain at age sixty, seventy, eighty, and beyond. You need only make the choice to educate your brain for a better way of life.

The Roaring Forties

For sailors, the phrase *roaring forties* refers to the area below forty degrees south latitude, where the ocean begins to become unrelentingly dangerous to small vessels because of huge seas and high winds. But for every man and woman, the term can also mean a time after age forty when the brain faces increasing danger of decline. New research has shown that in the brains of people in their forties, the parts of the brain involved in memory and cognitive function start losing their ability to function, at least in some people. Though studies are by no means conclusive, it suggests that in our fifth decade of life many of us may start experiencing physical brain breakdown without realizing it.

We do not see this as any surprise. After all, many of us have experienced difficulty remembering things in middle age—where we left the car keys, what we went into the kitchen to get, and so on. That the brain, like the rest of the body, undergoes some age-related change is not news. We lose between five and ten percent of our brain mass between the ages of twenty and eighty, and with that natural change comes some impairment, such as slower reaction time behind the wheel of a car, or failure to recall the name of a recent acquaintance. But although the aging brain naturally suffers some damage, dementia is not an unavoidable outcome of age. There is much you can do to prevent it.

Another commonly held myth about the aging brain is that our genetic inheritance puts our ultimate brain health beyond our control. We assume that because Aunt Sally forgot who she was by the time she was eighty-five, the same experience is likely in store for us. But was Aunt Sally obese? Did she exercise? What was her diet like? Did she learn new things as she got older, or did she stop learning? A raft of long-term research, particularly work carried out by the MacArthur Foundation, confirms that health that continues into old age is only fifteen to thirty percent determined by our genetic heritage. The remainder is mainly determined by our lifestyle choices and behaviors, psychology, environment, and life events.

Think for a moment about the implications. You are not powerless against your DNA. We all have the power to control at least seventy percent of our aging process through the lifelong choices we make in diet, exercise, mental health, learning, and relationships. We do not have to stand passively watching and hoping as our bodies and brains age, accepting the outcome as "just the way it is." We can make proactive, conscious choices to help our bodies and brains remain healthy and vital into our seventies, eighties, and nineties. That is a serious responsibility, but it also represents a wonderful hope for the future.

The Myths of Maturity

The reality is that old age by itself does not guarantee a loss of brain function. True, recent research shows that people with a certain gene are more likely to develop Alzheimer's disease or lose memory function. However, the same study shows that diabetes and heart disease carry the identical risk, and as we have said, these are diseases of lifestyle. It has become clear after decades of research that physical wellness, lifestyle, weight, diet, and exercise are far more important factors in brain health than genetics or age.

Age is not a choice; healthy living is. The lifestyle choices we make today play a large role in determining how sharp our minds and memories will be tomorrow.

Here are some other widespread myths related to the brain and age:

MYTH: SERIOUS BRAIN DECLINE IS INEVITABLE. Yes, changes in brain structure and chemistry do occur with age. But they do not have to lead to a steep decline in mental ability. Writing in *Newsweek*, Gene Cohen, M.D., Ph.D., founding director of the Center on Aging, Health, and Humanities at George Washington University Medical Center, says that in his work designing games to improve the mental function of aging men and women, he has found that the brain's left and right hemispheres (the left is responsible for linear, logical thinking; the right, for creativity and intuition) actually become better integrated as we age, leading to greater creative potential. Cohen writes that it is becoming clear that with the proper lifestyle and challenges, the brain can in many respects become stronger with age.

MYTH: I AM GETTING DUMBER BECAUSE MY BRAIN CELLS ARE DYING. It is true that brain cells die as we age. Brain cells die and new cells are born throughout our lives. But for many years people have assumed that, barring excessive drinking during college, brain cells cash in their chips at a higher rate as we get into the retirement years. But as it turns out, that is not true either. It appears that we lose brain cells at a consistent rate throughout life, owing to causes that range from stress and nutritional deficiencies to environmental toxins. Also, some neuroscientists now believe that brain cell death may be a part of the brain's learning process. The loss of some cells paves the way for new connections to develop as we learn, part of the sculpting of the brain that occurs when the brain remains active and constantly learning.

MYTH: THE ADULT BRAIN CANNOT FORM NEW CONNECTIONS. For many years, brain scientists were certain that the brain could not make new nerve cells to replace lost ones. But in the mid-1990s, researchers began to see evidence that indeed the brain can produce new nerve cells in some areas of the brain related to memory—a process called neurogenesis. This phenomenon is particularly responsive to regular physical exercise, meaning that working out is not just good for your heart, bones, and muscles, but good for your mind as well. Studies based on the work of Columbia University neurologist Scott Small and Salk Institute neurobiologist Fred Gage suggest that regular exercise delivers more oxygen-rich blood to the brain, as well as a chemical called *brain-derived neurotrophic factor*, or BDNF. These factors and others appear to improve memory, learning, and other brain functions.

Perhaps the most exciting discovery is that, like the rest of the body, brain vitality is a "use it or lose it" proposition. A recent study at the University of Pittsburgh School of Medicine shows that the more stimulating and intellectually challenging we make our lives, the better are our odds of keeping our aging brains vital, sharp, and agile. Just as with muscles, it appears that with lack of use our brains atrophy, failing to create new neural connections and replace dying brain cells.

Older people who follow the traditional path of retirement, sitting on the porch in a rocker and doing little or nothing, are inviting dementia and decline in brain function. By comparison, an enriched environment, as author and brain scientist Marion C. Diamond calls it—one filled with play, discovery, learning, and challenge—keeps the brain active and constantly producing new connective pathways. This quality, known as neuroplasticity, suggests that in the right environment our brains can evolve and change in wondrous ways throughout our lives.

So much for the idea that old dogs can't learn new tricks. Not only can they, but they should. Designing your life so that every day you are learning something new or looking at the world in a new way not only enhances brain health and mental activity but brings greater delight and satisfaction to living. What's good for your brain is also good for your soul.

Years of Peace, Giving, and Relationships

When we examine the leading neurological research, as well as our own professional and personal experience as observers of the brain and aging, we see a pattern emerging. As we age and our brains become slower as a result of dense neural growth and cell death, other factors compensate us. Most older adults can compensate for changes in brain function. A reduction in work demands means more opportunities to focus on relationships and on giving back to others, allowing a greater focus on happiness. Age brings wisdom, perspective, and reduced anxiety as we come to understand more about how life works and what is truly important—people, the natural world, beauty, peace, creativity, and joy. Aging may be difficult at times, but it is not without its rewards.

Imagine, then, if we started today to exercise and educate our brains and challenge ourselves to learn new things (for example, languages, musical instruments, or crafts). Imagine blending the wisdom and spiritual maturity of later life with a nimble, acute mind produced by years or decades of healthful brain education! We can combine the superior judgment of age with the mental acuity of youth. That would be quite a package, one that would transform our idea of what it means to age. This is precisely what the BEST method offers: a path to physical vigor, emotional peace, and personal meaning.

BEST's power to bring out the brain's best performance offers another benefit important to aging individuals: It can reduce the need for costly health care. As you will discover, BEST enlists body and mind in a program of exercise, meditation, mental challenge, and emotional cleansing.

If you follow this program, your brain and mind will enjoy improved overall health, enhanced sharpness, and reduced stress. BEST can help you delay or prevent the health problems so common to old age, keep you out of the hospital, and reduce your health care costs in an era when costs are rising and Medicare is at risk.

The Five Steps of
Brain Education System Training

BEST takes a different view of the brain from that of mainstream neuroscience. Though we acknowledge that neuroscience and neurobiology have made remarkable strides in understanding the physical function of this amazing organ, little is known to science about the way the brain creates conscious experience. So although many scientists take the reductive view that the mind is nothing more than the electrical and chemical processes of the brain, we hold a more holistic view that is integrated with frontier science but is also based on the personal experiences of its practitioners. To us, the brain is the remarkable organ that gives shape and application to the mind, which has its source in the oneness of existence that mystics and sages have spoken of for centuries.

The value of this view is that it gives you conscious control over your brain's development. Instead of being a powerless automaton controlled by the firings of your neurons, you can shape the way your brain evolves. BEST advises you to change the way you think about your brain. Instead of saying, "I am my brain," say, "I am the master of my brain." This thought instantly turns your brain into a finely tuned and complex instrument under your control. That will awaken and empower you, and your awakened self will become able to respond consciously instead of instinctively to the situations that arise in your life. You can live consciously and understand how the activity of your brain determines the nature of every interaction you have with people, objects, and experiences.

While we're at it, let's define the difference between the brain and the mind. The brain is the physical organ where much of the mind's activity takes place. The mind is not only the brain; rather, it exists in every cell of the body. It is a collection of conscious and unconscious processes that direct and influence our mental and physical behavior. The mind perceives, thinks, reasons, feels, wills, imagines, and desires. The brain is an energetic organ, using electrical impulses across its intricate neural web to let cells communicate and share information. In Brain Education System Training, you will learn exercises and practices designed to improve the flow of your brain energy and literally transform the way your brain functions. This may sound extraordinary, but that is only because you are not accustomed to thinking of your brain the way you think of a biceps or an abdominal muscle. Just like those body parts, your brain can be reshaped by consistent stimulation. If you have thought of your brain as something beyond influence because you cannot see or touch it, it's time to think in a new and exciting way.

Brain Education System Training has five steps, each building on the effect of the previous step to affect body, mind, and spirit. They are:

1. BRAIN SENSITIZING. As we have already discussed, exercise and brain vitality are intimately linked. You will discover the link between movement and brain development, focusing on muscle flexibility, joint health, abdominal exercises that improve digestive function, and exercises that awaken the five senses. This introductory step encourages brain awareness and awakens body and brain.

2. BRAIN VERSATILIZING. Your brain has the capacity to master new tasks throughout your life. This step leverages that capacity to help you improve your brain flexibility and free your brain from ingrained habits of thought. With challenging exercises and drills, you retrain your brain to operate in a more efficient, more effective way.

3. BRAIN REFRESHING. The negative thought patterns you may have spent your life establishing create a residue that blocks your potential and prevents deep emotional healing. Here, you will begin to release old traumas and unproductive emotions, to develop a more positive outlook, and to increase your emotional intelligence.

4. BRAIN INTEGRATING. At this level, the physical and emotional house-cleaning you have done has prepared you for the true work of BEST: integrating all the areas of your brain to craft a new identity unbounded by the ego, an identity that partakes of the true oneness of all things. With this deep work, you will begin to discover your life purpose and to release the creativity that has always been latent within you.

5. BRAIN MASTERING. Finally, you will continue to transform your brain and to establish and solidify new neural connections. This will lead you to a state of self-actualization, in which you partake of the peace you have granted yourself and the awareness of yourself as owner of your brain. As you continue to develop lifetime BEST habits, you will become more decisive and find yourself forming more lasting, fulfilling relationships.

Based on a blend of yoga-like exercise, meditation (a tool for mental and emotional growth, not a religious practice), challenging physical movement, and stimulating intellectual drills, BEST is a ground-breaking discipline perfect for people with the desire to live into their mature years not only more healthfully, but with more joy, love, and self-awareness. With the added insight of today's latest gerontological and neurological science, this approach can become not a fountain of youth, but a fountain of vitality for many decades to come.

Your BEST Moments

Before we move on to the steps of BEST, a word of wisdom about changing the way you think right now. One of the blessings of the aging brain is that you have a deep reservoir of existing knowledge that helps you gain immediate perspective on a situation.

This means that you have the insight to savor a particular moment in time, a kind of insight that a younger person often lacks. Whereas young people are usually looking toward the future and the next hurdle with little regard for the present, your time-tested perspective allows you to pause and truly be in the moment, which is where all of life's true delights arise. But this is not a characteristic restricted to those of retirement age. No matter what your age, you can train your mind to perceive and live in the moment. In part, that is what BEST is all about: extracting all the learning, delight, and peace each moment has to offer, then moving on to the next.

Training your brain to approach life in this way will make your maturity a marvelous adventure. Instead of experiencing a decline, you will relish the vivacity that few people of any age genuinely experience, because you will have made the most of your brain's unlimited potential.

The Jangsaeng Lifestyle

The word *jangsaeng* is a Korean word that roughly translates as "longevity." However, the word in English does not quite carry the same connotation. For us, longevity primarily means long life in respect to passage of time. But the Korean word suggests not only living many years, but also living them in a truly vital way. Jangsaeng person carry a youthful vitality into their older years that may be otherwise missing in their peers. To have Jangsaeng, you must have much more than long life. Jangsaeng people have a spring in their step and twinkle in their eye that is an inspiration even to the youngest ones around them.

In the West, we have done much to promote longevity. People today are living longer and longer as Western medicine advances. But extended life span should not be the only goal. It is more important that we live more fulfilling, happy lives, not just longer lives. This book exists to promote Jangsaeng, a lifestyle that promotes a positive, healthy living through awareness and utilization of the brain.

In the appendix, you will find a description of Jangsaeng Walking (page 179), a way of walking that keeps the body and the brain energized and youthful. This is one example of how the things we do everyday, such as walking, have great impact on the quality of life. All the information in this book is meant to promote the Jangsaeng lifestyle by helping people get the most out of their brains in their later years. Please use it to create a Jangsaeng Brain and a Jangsaeng Life.

FIVE HEALTHY HABITS FOR AN AGING BRAIN

1. EXERCISE REGULARLY.

Brisk cardiovascular exercise brings rich, oxygenated blood to the brain. You should get at least 30 minutes of heart-pumping exercise 3 times a week. Also, do strength training at least twice a week, because muscle development also produces more energy for the brain.

2. REDUCE STRESS.

Stress is a major cause of illness, thanks to the effects of the hormone cortisol. Too much cortisol can wear down the hippocampus, which plays a role in memory function. Exercise and meditation can help.

3. GET PLENTY OF SLEEP.

Sleep deprivation is the number one cause of fuzzy, disjointed mental function. Studies show that people who get at least eight hours of sleep each night can avoid some age-related brain decline.

4. EAT LOW-FAT AND HEALTHY.

Glucose spikes and fatty plaque deposits that accompany overeating can damage the brain. A lower-calorie diet promotes better circulation and also controls weight, leading to lower blood pressure.

5. GIVE YOUR BRAIN A WORKOUT.

Try to do or learn something new each week, whether you are writing a letter with the hand you do not usually use or developing your knowledge of a new language. Challenging the brain with novel tasks and activities creates new neural pathways, makes it more versatile, and improves its multitasking ability.

Young Brain Quiz

There are no right or wrong answers to this short quiz, because there is nothing you are doing today that cannot be improved tomorrow. However, it is important to know where you stand today in maintaining and even enhancing your brain's vitality. Complete each of the sections and then look at the end for your score.

YOUR BODY AND BRAIN

1. I get strenuous exercise (at least thirty minutes)...

   a) 5–6 times per week.

   b) 3–4 times per week.

   c) 1–2 times per week.

   d) I love my couch.

2. I stretch my limbs and joints ...

   a) 5–6 times per week.

   b) 3–4 times per week.

   c) 1–2 times per week.

   d) The only thing I stretch is the truth.

3. My typical diet is ...

   a) 7–10 servings of fruit and vegetables per day, lots of whole grains, low fat, not much alcohol or red meat.

   b) 4–6 servings of fruit and vegetables per day, some whole grains, moderate fat, some red meat.

   c) Refined grains, red meat often, and few fruits and vegetables.

   d) I recognize four food groups: fast, frozen, junk, and spoiled.

4. I sleep ...

    a) At least 8 hours just about every night.

    b) 6-7 hours most nights.

    c) Well some nights, poorly others.

    d) I'm a connoisseur of 3 a.m. infomercials.

PUTTING YOUR BRAIN TO WORK

1. I read ...

    a) Constantly, usually challenging material.

    b) 2-3 times per week; sometimes books, sometimes magazines.

    c) Once in a while, when I'm on vacation.

    d) Never; I'm too busy watching TV.

2. I try to learn new skills or hobbies, such as a musical instrument or a language ...

    a) Whenever I have free time.

    b) When I'm feeling bored.

    c) Rarely.

    d) I guess I'm too comfortable, because I haven't tried such things in years.

3. I engage in puzzles, Sudoku, or other brain-challenging activities ...

    a) Daily.

    b) A few times a week.

    c) Once in a while.

    d) My brain is challenged enough when I try to play a movie on my DVD player.

4. When I am in conversation, I like ...

a) Deep, intense talks about complex issues with people who challenge my perceptions with new information.

b) Some debate, but usually nothing heavy.

c) People who agree with me.

d) I don't enjoy conversation much.

BALANCING YOUR BRAIN

1. When it comes to my interests and passions, I ...

a) Pursue what I love as my main vocation.

b) Balance earning a living with doing what I enjoy.

c) Wish I had more time for the things I care about.

d) Have no idea what my passions are.

2. During stressful times ...

a) I keep my perspective, meditate, stay healthy, and/or give love to others.

b) I can get a little stressed out, but I'm pretty good about breathing and letting it wash away.

c) I can internalize stress, and sometimes I let a stressful situation ruin my day.

d) I lose my temper easily under stress, and my friends have nick-named me Vesuvius.

3. My outlook on life tends to be that ...

a) Everything happens for a reason and we're all okay.

b) Most people in general are good, and the world will probably be all right.

c) We've got a lot of problems, and I don't know whether human kind will make it.

d) I'm scared to death of what will happen in the near future.

4. Having a full calendar of things to do makes me feel ...

a) Delighted; I love being busy as long as I have downtime as well!

b) Good, though I also get a little overwhelmed.

c) That I wish I were busier.

d) I spend a lot of time at home by myself.

LIFE AND YOUR BRAIN

1. I have control over ...

a) The conditions of my life.

b) My attitude toward life.

c) Very little; everything seems pretty random.

d) Nothing.

2. Describe the way you feel about your current career or volunteer work:

a) I'm lucky to do what I do.

b) I like my work, but I'm not leaping out of bed every morning.

c) I'd like to do something else, but what?

d) I'm retired and the question doesn't apply to me.

3. Describe the kinds of goals you set for yourself:

a) I set ambitious goals, and I love pushing myself.

b) I set realistic goals that I'm somewhat sure I can achieve.

c) I'm not a big goal setter; I have no follow-through.

d) I just go where the wind blows me.

4. When it comes to aging, I ...

    a) Plan to live an exciting, healthy life filled with love, wisdom, and discovery.

    b) Plan on staying active, traveling, and giving back to others.

    c) Am not sure what to expect, and I feel a little anxiety.

    d) Am terrified about disease and dementia.

. . . .

SCORING

How did you do? Remember, there are no right answers—just a sketch of where you are today. The fact that you are reading this book means that you are ready to take yourself from where you are now to a new level of brain awareness and growing wisdom. On to your scores. For each "a" answer, give yourself four points; for each "b," three; two for each "c,"; and one for each "d."

55–64 POINTS: You are very healthy and probably already engage in many of the practices in this book in some way. With a little fine tuning, your future is limitless.

40–54 POINTS: You're part of the majority of people reading this book. You have some limits on your thinking and your lifestyle, but you also have great potential. It won't take long for you to vault into your fulfilling life.

26–39 POINTS: You're not feeling, looking, thinking, or doing your best, and you know it. You're probably angry with yourself, but try to forgive. Nobody is perfect, and there is much you can do to improve your health, outlook, and mind.

16–25 POINTS: You've been allowing yourself to neglect everything that matters, from your health to your job to your future. You have to make some changes fast. Fortunately, you are reading the right book.

THE SENIOR FITNESS TEST

The preceding Young Brain Quiz is not a scientifically designed assessment. Rather it is simply a fun self-assessment that is meant to help you to see your own habits and attitudes more clearly. If you would like to try a scientifically validated test, try the Senior Fitness Test on page 210 of the appendix. It is very easy to do, and through it you can see exactly how you measure up in comparison to other adults your age. It was developed in the process of testing more than seven thousand older adults for strength, balance, and flexibility. Created through the work of Jessie Jones, Ph.D., and her colleagues, it is one of the most widely recognized and commonly utilized methods in the world for determining senior fitness. Test yourself once before you begin BEST training, and then retest after three to six months.

CHAPTER 1

Your Sensitized Brain

It is not enough to have a good mind; the main thing is to use it well.
—René Descartes

On March 26, 2007, *Newsweek* ran a fascinating article about the connection between exercise and brain performance. It explained that according to Charles Hillman, a University of Illinois professor of neurology and kinesiology, those who engage in regular exercise have fitter brains in addition to fitter bodies.

Brain Sensitizing, the first part of Brain Education System Training, ties into this idea. It uses specially designed exercises with which one can awaken the senses, develop a keener sense of energy flow, and gain a greater awareness of the brain's functioning. These activities are foundational to your health and to your progress through the BEST method, so please make them a regular part of your daily routine.

The Benefits of Exercise

For decades, during most of what comprises the history of modern Western medicine, it has been assumed that once a person reached adulthood, that was the end of increasing brain function. Brain cells, they thought, would begin to die rapidly starting in the forties and would continue to shuffle off this mortal coil; there was little anyone could do about it. However, it turns out that the conventional wisdom (as often proves to be the case) was wrong: the brain can indeed form new neural connections—in a process called neurogenesis—leading to faster communication and greater ability to learn and remember. The brain can and does continue to improve throughout life. There are many possible ways to improve various aspects of brain performance, but physical exercise is one of the best ways to take advantage of this marvelous brain ability.

Until recently, most scientists believed that the positive effects of exercise came about largely as the result of increased blood flow to the brain. Although a boost in circulation certainly has its benefits, as it brings more oxygenated blood to the brain, the complete picture is more interesting. It appears that with each movement in rigorous exercise, the muscle releases a hormone that stimulates the growth of new nerves in the brain's learning and memory center. So when you exercise, you're ordering the brain to produce more cells and more connections. No one knows yet whether new cells can grow in the rest of the brain as a result of exercise, but there is little doubt that the entire brain thrives on the extra blood and oxygen that flood it when we hit the elliptical machine, lift weights, or swim a few laps in the community pool.

Being Fit Above the Neck

For all the many ways in which exercise benefits mental function, we cannot directly exercise our frontal lobe in the same way as we can extend a triceps muscle or stretch a hamstring. Therefore, it becomes easy to ignore the link between personal fitness and the health and vigor of the brain. The truth, as we see in the *Newsweek* story, is that the physical body and the health of the brain are intimately connected, and this becomes truer as we age.

As you are probably aware, exercise is widely accepted by medical science as a key factor in maintaining health and well-being throughout the aging process. In fact, it may be the most important aspect of successful aging. Most of the physical effects of aging—the natural loss of muscle mass, the decreased flexibility and mobility of joints, the decline of metabolism that can lead to weight gain—can be prevented or even reversed through regular moderate exercise. Exercise helps prevent heart disease; staves off obesity, which can lead to diabetes; is one of our best defenses against cancer; and, as we have seen above, improves brain function. Exercise is the most powerful health care you can give your body, and unless you overdo it and pull a muscle, it has no side effects.

Brain Sensitizing leverages the power of exercise to benefit the brain. Our goal is to teach you to reestablish that connection between your body and your brain—to help you become more aware of the way your brain interacts with the rest of your body and the way each movement stimulates a different area of your brain. Even more important, we will help you awaken your five senses, the most direct way your brain interacts with the physical world. Through basic energy meditation techniques and breathing work, you will also learn to develop stronger concentration and awareness of the life force within you, and you will restore a healthy balance of that energy throughout your body. The serenity and clarity that you will experience after even a short period of Brain Sensitizing practice will make spending that time worthwhile.

A Word About Ki

In the following chapters, you will encounter the term *Ki*. To the mind steeped in Western science, the concept of Ki (also spelled chi or qi), or life energy, can seem archaic and even superstitious. Isn't Ki just an Asian myth? Hasn't it been disproved by Western science? Such questions are natural, and it is important that you know the facts about this ancient concept before proceeding, since it is integral to the BEST method. If you are skeptical, that is good. Open-minded skepticism is a sign of wisdom.

The concept of Ki includes the idea that all living beings contain a circulating life energy that flows through the body along meridians. From the viewpoint of traditional Asian medicine, disease and distress are largely the results of imbalances of positive and negative energies. Ki is the foundation of all traditional Asian medical practice. But is it real, or merely a metaphor appropriate only to Chinese, Japanese, and Korean folk medicine? Some scientists are quick to dismiss Ki as a concept that does not fit into any accepted models of how the body or brain works. However, tightly controlled experiments have begun to demonstrate that Ki is a real force with real effects. A rigorous experiment carried out in 2001 and published in the *Ameri-*

can *Journal of Chinese Medicine* shows that Ki masters and Ki trainees can produce changes in human blood cells. Other experiments have demonstrated the fact that Ki energy can be measured. A growing body of evidence shows that Ki is a very real force.

BEST sees Ki as the connecting element between mind and body. In other words, Ki is the thing that allows the mind to affect the body. The validity of the mind-body connection was confirmed in the 1950s when biofeedback researchers discovered that people could easily learn to change their heart rate, body temperature, and other physiological functions.

The principles and practices of BEST depend not on belief, but on execution and dedication. Many people have experienced this energy personally and benefited from its effects. As you progress through the work of BEST, you may use disciplines that will enable you to feel the power of Ki energy in your body. We advise you to trust these sensations rather than worry about whether they have been approved by Western science. There are many ways to know that something is valid; personal experience is one of them. We respect science, but we also revere the personal journey of every human being. If you keep an open mind and approach this work with commitment and self-awareness, you will see results.

Good for the Body, Good for the Brain

There are four major kinds of exercise that older people should engage in to keep their brains stimulated and their bodies vigorous and active. You should include the following in your routine for maximum brain health:

1. AEROBIC EXERCISE. Also called cardio, aerobic exercise gets the heart pumping, which helps oxygen and nutrients to flow throughout the body, so it is ideal for achieving weight loss and helping keep the heart and other organs healthy. Aerobic activities counter some well-known age-related physiological changes, reverse disuse syndrome, control chronic diseases, and maximize brain function. Common aerobic activities are walking or hiking, cycling, swimming, treadmills, step machines, and dance classes.

2. RESISTANCE TRAINING. Also known as strength training, this type of exercise requires the body's muscles to move against an opposing force or resistance, whether you are lifting your own weight with push-ups or sit-ups, or using free weights, resistance bands, or weight machines. Over time, resistance training can not only reverse most age-related muscle loss, but can also lower the risk of diabetes, hypertension, and osteoporosis, and it improves posture, balance, and the overall function of the organs. One more benefit of resistance training that many people are unaware of is that the more muscle you have, the faster your metabolism is.

3. FLEXIBILITY TRAINING. Although some age-related change in flexibility is inevitable, much of the decline can be countered through daily flexibility exercises. Exercises that stretch the muscles help to reduce muscle pain and injury, and to improve muscle function, mobility (for example, bending to pick up something, reaching overhead, or washing your back), and posture. In addition to the more traditional flexibility exercises, other ways to improve your joints' range of motion include participating in challenging activities, such as tai chi, Pilates, yoga, and martial arts.

4. BALANCE AND MOBILITY TRAINING. Balance and mobility training is a critical component of an exercise program that is often ignored. Falls are the leading cause of injury for people sixty-five and over. Our brain education program helps to address some of the sensory, cognitive, and motor components associated with dynamic balance and mobility.

As you proceed through the book, you will see that BEST focuses primarily on exercises related to numbers three and four above. This is due to the specific brain-enhancing features of these exercises. However, you should still seek out aerobic and resistance training for the overall health of the body and brain. Jangsaeng Walking, detailed on page 179 of the appendix, is a good general conditioning exercise rooted in the principles of Ki.

Exercise has many benefits for us as we age, but they are not only benefits to muscles, joints, bones, and the waistline. Regular physical activity can improve brain function, attitude, self-image, self-esteem, and confidence. You've heard of the "runner's high"? Well, it's no myth. When you exercise, you stimulate the release of biochemicals such as endorphins, norepinephrine, dopamine, and serotonin, which produce feelings of joy and peace. Healthy exercise feels great.

The true benefits accrue to us as we age. Regular exercise has been shown to help alleviate depression in people over fifty, who can be prone to negative feelings as they face illnesses, empty nests, retirement, and the deaths of loved ones. In fact, regular workouts have been shown to have a stronger antidepressant effect than prescription drugs. Exercise also helps prevent obesity, a problem that is rampant in the United States. and can lead to a number of other very serious diseases, from arthritis and diabetes to heart disease and stroke. In fact, the four major killers in this country—heart disease, stroke, diabetes, and cancer—are largely diseases of lifestyle. Change your lifestyle to reduce your risk of developing these serious conditions.

In general, no matter who you are, you will experience positive effects from regular exercise. These can include stronger bones, which can ward off osteoporosis; an increased range of joint motion; increased strength and the ability to perform physical work; lower blood pressure; better blood sugar balance, which can prevent or reverse diabetes; improved sleep; and possibly even an improved sex drive. There is a subculture of people who rely on injections of human growth hormone, or HGH, to achieve some of these benefits. HGH occurs naturally in the body but decreases starting in your twenties and throughout the rest of your life; its reduction is thought to be a major cause of the loss of muscle mass, slower metabolism, and lowered sex drive in older adults. But HGH is extremely expensive, costing tens of thousands of dollars per year, and it can have serious side effects. Still, it fits many people's desire to find a quick fix for the effects of aging. Needless to say, we think exercise is a far wiser and healthier choice for people seeking to be physically and mentally fit in later life.

Contrary to a common myth, exercise is safe for older people. You should always check with your physician before beginning an exercise regimen to make sure you do not have a heart problem or other condition that would make exercise hazardous. Also, getting some guidance from a personal trainer with experience in training older adults would be wise. As long as you do not overtrain and injure yourself, there is no area of your body that will not take to regular exercise like a duck to water—especially your brain.

Food and Your Brain

This book would not be complete without a few words about the foods that are beneficial for your brain. The foods you eat, of course, have a direct effect on your health and wellness, and many Americans consume far too much sodium, saturated fat, and processed ingredients, which contribute to circulatory blockages that deny the brain its blood supply and cause high blood pressure and other conditions detrimental to brain health.

In general, a diet rich in fresh foods, fruits, vegetables, and whole grains is as good for your brain as it is for the rest of your body. However, there are certain foods that pack more punch for the brain than others:

- Foods rich in Omega-3 fatty acids, such as salmon, tuna, and walnuts
- Foods rich in the B vitamin choline, such as eggs
- Sources of good fats, such as avocados, almonds, or extra-virgin olive oil
- Green leafy vegetables, dried legumes, and lean meats, which provide vital amino acids
- Whole-grain breads, cereals, and crackers

The Work of Brain Sensitizing

Brain Sensitizing is an integrated mind-body training method that focuses on stimulating specific areas of the brain, eliminating blockages to the flow of Ki energy, and quieting the mind through deep stretching, meditative breathing techniques, and energy awareness. As a tool for meditation, improved concentration and awareness, and greater physical well-being, it is perfect for older people seeking a healing, holistic way to promote brain health and overall health.

This work often takes the form of yoga, but even if you integrate meditation or other disciplines into your practice, Brain Sensitization gives practitioners a way to get off the merry-go-round of life and to listen to their true selves, promoting inner peace and a rediscovery of purpose and meaning in life—something of great value to older people facing retirement, physical decline, or the uncertainty of life in an ever-changing world.

Brain Sensitizing exercises promote the body-brain connection and recognize the brain as the center of the human body, perception, and experience. People who do these exercises learn to use their brains more fully for the creation of a better life. This is a practice that recognizes the power of the mind and spirit to heal the body. Using the exercises in this book, you will learn to master the use of your own inner energy and to enhance your physical, mental, and spiritual wellness.

The effectiveness of Brain Sensitizing is based on the control of a fundamental principle of life as it is known in traditional Asian medicine. The idea that cool water energy and hot fire energy flow freely in our bodies is known as su-seung-hwa-gang, which means "water up, fire down." When the body is in balance, cool water energy travels upward, toward the head and hot fire energy flows down to the lower abdomen—the "fire in the belly." This mirrors the cycle of water and fire in nature, as the heat of the sun evaporates the water of oceans and rivers, which eventually falls back to earth as rain. When the natural flow of these opposites is in balance, with the water energy flowing toward the head along the back of the body and fire energy flowing down along the front of the body, mind and body feel at peace and well. When this flow is out of balance, nothing feels right. Digestion is not working well, emotions feel out of control and disconnected, and pain is common. Brain Sensitizing works to balance these opposing forces.

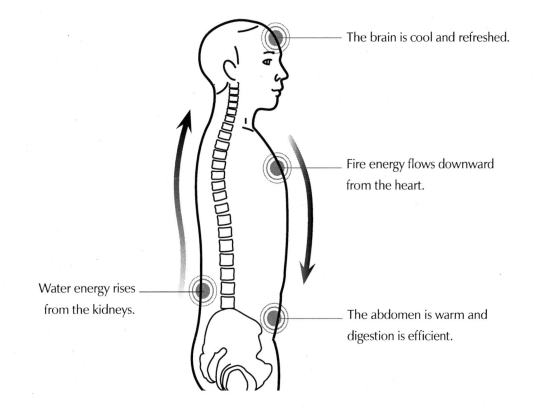

The brain is cool and refreshed.

Fire energy flows downward from the heart.

Water energy rises from the kidneys.

The abdomen is warm and digestion is efficient.

The State of "Water Up, Fire Down"

The Stress Connection

Looking from the Western perspective, Brain Sensitizing works to restore proper balance between two systems—the sympathetic and parasympathetic nervous systems. In other words, it works to relieve the effects of the stress response, which has been concretely linked to so many of today's common health problems.

Stress is of particular concern in the area of brain health, due to its effect on learning and overall brain function. In small doses, the chemical cascade associated with the fight-or-flight response can be good for the brain, motivating us to act and keeping us on our toes. But when we get a constant stream of stress hormones, as is often the case for people today, it can wear down on mental function, especially in the area of memory and mental acuity. Over time, this can result in truly debilitating effects on brain performance. Through Brain Sensitizing activities, you can learn to regulate the effects of stress, returning your body and brain to the rest-and-digest state of being.

Creating New Pathways to Health

Brain Sensitizing consists of three key practices. The first involves stretching exercises of the kind often found in yoga, Pilates, tai chi, or martial arts. As each muscle of your body is activated in deep stretching poses, corresponding areas of your brain awaken, improving coordination and balance. The second practice involves breathing methods combined with dynamic body positioning, again often part of meditative practices and yoga. Finally, there is basic energy meditation. This practice encourages you to view Ki energy as the link between body and mind, expanding your awareness and increasing brain clarity. Many practitioners find they are able to begin changing negative habits using this technique.

For older Americans, the loss of cognitive abilities because of some form of dementia is a greater source of fear than even the possibility of a heart attack or a stroke. Yet most neuroscientists agree that the human brain has the capacity to function beautifully past our 100th birthday. Then what makes the difference between the eighty-year-old man who cannot remember his children and the woman of 102 who paints and writes poetry when she's not competing in the Senior Olympics? Regularly exercising the brain's "muscles"–the neural connections, or dendrites, that support cognition, imagination, and creativity. Brain Sensitizing helps to counteract the mental decline associated with aging by providing natural stress relief and eliminating blockages of Ki energy.

Brain Sensitizing sparks the creation of new neural pathways in the brain, awakening underused areas of both the left and the right hemisphere in order to keep the centers of learning, information processing, and memory sound and thriving. As brain cells die, this process helps to replace them. Practitioners also find they are better able to exercise control over their brains, transforming lifelong patterns of thinking, breaking bad habits, and letting go of ingrained prejudices. In the end, your goal should be a brain that is peaceful, creative, and productive. As Dr. David Myers says in his book *The Pursuit of Happiness*, "Well-being is found in the renewal of a disciplined lifestyle, and the giving and receiving of acceptance."

Proper Stance

When you are exercising, you should make sure you have good posture and alignment. Through the years, your body has probably developed habits that are less than ideal. If you conscientiously strive to improve your posture, you are essentially retraining your brain to adopt a healthier habit. When you do the standing exercises suggested in this book, try to keep this posture.

As with any physical exercise, be careful not to exceed your body's limitations. Remember—you don't have to be perfect. Practice consistently and you will improve one step at a time.

Shoulders: Relax your shoulders.

Waist: Straighten your waist and curl your tailbone inward like a hook. When you curl the tailbone, the S-curve of the spine is straightened and a gentle strain is present in the lower abdomen.

Knees: Bend your knees slightly and naturally. Avoid locking the knees, because this can block the energy flow.

Legs: Spread your legs at shoulder width. Spreading the legs too wide can scatter the energy in the lower abdomen and lower body.

Feet: Place your feet parallel to each other, in the shape of the number eleven. Spread the feet no more than shoulder width to avoid losing the energy stored in the lower abdomen.

Soles: Balance your body weight evenly on both soles.

Breathing: When you stretch, focus your mind on an area where you feel pain. Inhale gently through the nose and imagine healing energy flowing to that part of your body. Open the mouth slightly and exhale naturally, and feel the blockage being released from your body.

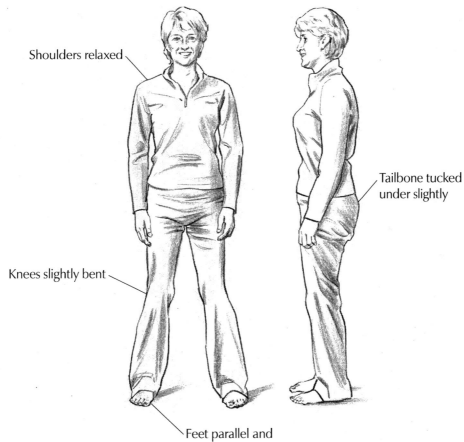

Shoulders relaxed

Tailbone tucked under slightly

Knees slightly bent

Feet parallel and shoulder width apart

Body Opening Exercises

This group of exercises will help you keep your body loose and relaxed. Many of them focus on keeping the joints functioning smoothly, which is very important for lifelong mobility. This is also absolutely essential for brain health, because inactivity leads directly to the decline of the brain. You have probably heard the saying, "Use it or lose it." We might revise that to read "Use your body or lose your brain." These exercises can be used for basic body and brain maintenance, and to help keep the effects of time at bay.

BOUNCE 'N' SWEEP

Use this simple technique to quickly release tension from your body, especially from around the shoulders and upper back. You can imagine that you are sweeping stress out of your body as you bounce up and down.

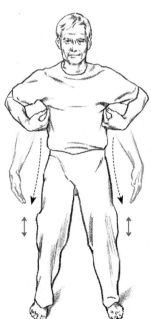

1. Stand with your feet shoulder width apart and your feet parallel.
2. Bring the backs of your fingers under your armpits.
3. Quickly sweep down the sides of your body as you bend your knees slightly.
4. Repeat this movement 10 to 20 times in quick succession, creating a bouncing, rhythmic motion.

ARM FLING

This simple, enjoyable movement helps to release tension from the body. While doing it, try to imagine that you have the loose, carefree body of a child as you bounce up and down.

1. Relax your shoulders and bend your knees slightly.
2. Keep your feet planted on the floor beneath your shoulders as you swing your arms side to side.
3. Bounce your knees to the rhythm of the movement.
4. Repeat 20 or more times.

WHOLE-BODY TAPPING

This exercise is designed to improve circulation throughout your body. Circulation is critical for delivering fresh, oxygenated blood to your brain. Also, every time you pat a particular area of your body, a corresponding part of your brain is stimulated. Try to follow the order given here because it works with the natural circulation of the body.

❶ Form your fingers into a cup and lightly tap over your head and face. Stretch out your left arm with your palm facing up. Take your right hand and, starting from the left shoulder, pat rhythmically downward all the way to the left hand.

❷ Then turn your left hand over and with your right hand, pat your way back up to the left shoulder again. Repeat tapping with the left hand and on the right arm.

❸ Pat your chest with both hands several times, breathing deeply and exhaling completely. Moving on from your chest, pat your ribs, abdomen, and sides. With both hands, pat the area just below the right rib cage, where your liver is located, and concentrate on radiating positive, clear energy to the liver.

❹ With both hands, tap the area just below the left rib cage, where your stomach is located, and concentrate on bringing healing energy to your stomach.

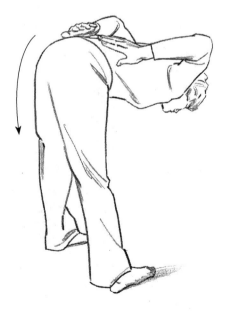

❺ Bend over slightly from the waist and pat your lower back (on both sides), where your kidneys are located, and move up, tapping as far as your hands can reach. Then tap your way down to your buttocks.

❻ Starting from your buttocks, pat your way down the backs of your legs to your ankles.

7 From the ankles, start patting your way up the fronts of your legs until you reach your upper thighs.

8 From your upper thighs, pat your way down the outsides of your legs to your ankles.

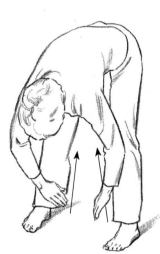

9 From the ankles, pat your way up the insides of your legs to your upper thighs.

10 Finish by striking your lower abdomen about 20 times.

SHOULDER ROTATION

This exercise will help you keep your shoulder joints open. It will also help you relax the muscles around your shoulder blades, which often hide knots of tension.

1. Put both hands on the shoulders and stretch the elbows forward.
2. Lift your elbows to shoulder height.
3. Make a large circular motion and rotate them slowly once.
4. Repeat 6 times front to back and 6 times back to front.

PELVIC ROTATION

You can think of this exercise as your daily hula lesson. It will help you keep your hip joints and lower back relaxed. Aloha!

1. Stand with your feet parallel and your legs spread at shoulder width. Place your hands on your hips. Keep your knees straight.
2. Rotate your hips in a large circle, pushing as far as you can in all directions. Repeat 5 times and then reverse and do 5 in the opposite direction.

HIP JOINT ROTATION

This exercise helps strengthen the hips, buttocks, and hamstrings. If you, like a lot of people, have spent a great deal of time sitting in chairs, you may lack mobility in the hip joints. This exercise helps to correct this problem.

1. Relax the upper body and gently curl the tailbone while standing up straight. At the same time, create firm but gentle tension in the lower abdomen. Hold onto a stable object, such as a chair or wall, if you need it for balance.

2. In an "at ease" posture, lift the right knee up to the lower abdomen level and rotate it outward 30 times.

3. Change legs and do the same thing 30 times.

4. Again, lift the right knee and rotate it 30 times in the opposite direction. Change legs and do the same thing 30 times.

KNEE ROTATION

Knee problems are among the most common physical complaints as we get older. Use this exercise to help prepare your knees for any strenuous activity.

1. Bend your knees slightly and keep the bottoms of your feet flat on the floor. Rest your hands on your knees, but do not put any weight on your knees with your hands. Relax your upper body.

2. Rotate your knees, together, in a circular motion toward the right. Do not raise the bottoms of your feet off the floor.

3. Repeat the movement, circling in the opposite direction.

4. Rotate your knees in little circles, inside to outside, allowing your knees to separate slightly.

5. Repeat the movement in the opposite direction, outside to inside.

ABDOMINAL TAPPING

This exercise may seem a little strange at first, but it is very effective to bring circulation to the internal organs. It will also help you keep centered within your body.

As you rhythmically pat the lower abdomen with the palms of both hands, blood and energy are distributed throughout the body. Abdominal exercises assist in the prompt removal of excess gases and waste from the body, and you will feel increased warmth in the lower abdomen as well.

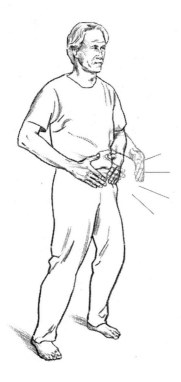

❶ Spread your feet at shoulder width and bend your knees slightly.

❷ Point your toes slightly inward; you will feel a slight tightening of the lower abdomen.

❸ Rhythmically strike the lower abdomen area with both palms.

❹ Begin with 100 strikes. You may increase the number and force of the strikes with more practice.

INTESTINE EXERCISE

A great deal of tension may be held in the abdomen, which is one reason many people develop digestive troubles. Use this exercise to help release tension and to improve intestinal function. Although this exercise is shown in a standing position, it can also be done seated or lying down.

❶ Stand with your feet shoulder width apart.

❷ Place your thumbs on your navel with your hands forming an upside-down triangle.

❸ Keeping your upper body relaxed, pull your abdomen inward.

❹ Now push your abdomen out, making it round like a balloon.

❺ Repeat this motion several times, working up to 100 or more repetitions.

Stretching Exercises

Brain health depends to a large extent on proper circulation in the body. The best way to maintain circulation is through flexibility and mobility. Create the habit of stretching your entire body every day to make both your body and brain healthier.

If you find that you are not quite as flexible as you used to be, be patient with yourself. These exercises do not have to be performed perfectly to be effective, and you will have great improvement with consistent practice.

NECK STRETCH

The neck is one of the most likely parts of the skeleton to become mis-aligned. If you have ever had a stiff neck, you probably know how important it is to maintain neck alignment. This exercise is great for helping you keep your neck in balanced alignment, which is often changed for the worse by the things we habitually do.

❶ Move only your neck and head, very slowly. Relax the rest of your body. Stretch your neck backward, pushing your chin upward.

❷ Bend your head sideways to the left and try to touch your left ear to your shoulder.

③ Repeat this movement in the opposite direction, trying to touch your right ear to your right shoulder.

④ Slowly turn your head to the left.

⑤ Repeat this movement in the opposite direction, turning your head to the right.

⑥ Next, rotate your head to the left.

⑦ Repeat this movement in the opposite direction.

SHOULDER STRETCH

This is a great exercise for rejuvenation at any time. Not only does it help you release tension held in your shoulders and upper back, but it opens your chest for easier breathing.

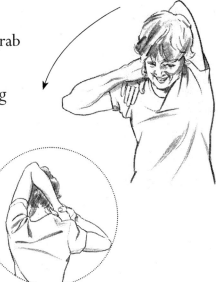

❶ Place one arm behind your head and grab your wrist with your opposite hand.

❷ Pull down on your wrist while pushing the elbow up above the head.

❸ Breathe in and push back on your arm with your head.

❹ Hold this position for about 5 counts and then release. Repeat on the opposite side.

REACH-UP

This stretch helps balance both sides of your body, which is ultimately related to balance between the left and right hemisheres of your brain. It also stretches and opens parts of your chest that are normally static.

1. Place your right foot forward and your right palm on your right thigh.
2. Inhale and reach behind your head with your left hand, your palm facing the ceiling. Let your head drop back as you follow the movement of the hand with your eyes.
3. Exhale and slowly return to the original position.
4. Repeat 3 times and then repeat on the opposite side of the body.

WRIST TWIST

This motion helps you keep your wrists open and can help you prevent carpal tunnel syndrome. In addition, it is a good challenge for the brain.

❶ Extend your left arm straight out in front of your chest and twist your palm so that it faces outward toward the left.

❷ Place your right palm on the left palm and clasp your hands together.

❸ Keeping your palms tightly clasped, bring your hands down toward your abdomen, bending your elbows.

❹ Lift your clasped hands toward your chest and upward between your arms and extend them out as straight as you can. Hold this position for 10 counts.

❺ Return and repeat on the opposite side.

SIDE STRETCH

In addition to giving you a satisfying stretch of the muscles all along the side of the body, this posture will also help you improve blood circulation to the organs in the abdomen.

1. Place your left hand on your left leg. Inhale, and at the same time reach the right hand over the ear toward the left side. Allow your left hand to slide down your leg to a comfortable position. Try to keep your body upright without bending forward.
2. Hold this position for 3 counts. Exhale and slowly return to your original position.
3. Repeat 3 times on each side of the body.

FORWARD BEND

Your legs, especially the hamstrings, can tighten up very quickly if you do not stretch them regularly. Do this exercise every day and you will be touching your toes in no time.

1. Sit with your legs together, stretched straight out in front of you.
2. Place your hands on your knees. Move your arms in a circular motion toward the backs of your hips, circling them up over your head.
3. Bend your torso and lower back so that your hands can touch your toes.
4. Concentrate on keeping your legs straight while you bend at the elbow, bringing your chest and head toward your knees. Hold this position for about 10 counts, and then return to your original posture.
5. Repeat this exercise several times.

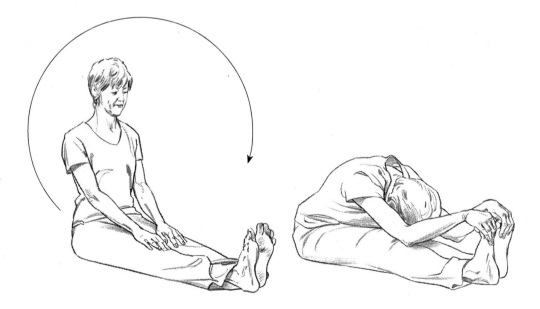

HIP STRETCH

If you are like most people, you have probably spent too much time sitting during your life. This exercise will help you open up your hip joints and possibly help you avoid injury in the future.

❶ Lie comfortably on the floor. Bend one knee and grasp your shin with your hands.

❷ Pull your knee in toward your chest and down toward your armpit.

❸ Inhale and hold your breath for 5 counts, then release as you exhale.

❹ Repeat this motion 3 times on each side.

INNER THIGH STRETCH

If you have not regularly made an effort to stretch your inner thighs, you may find this exercise difficult at first. To avoid injury, start with only a light stretch and work up to a deeper one.

❶ Keeping your feet parallel, spread your feet widely, about twice your shoulder width. Place your hands on your hips or hold onto a stable object.

❷ Bend one knee and lower your hips toward the floor while keeping the unbent leg extended.

❸ Adjust your stance as needed to achieve a solid stretch in the inner thigh. Hold for 10 counts.

❹ Repeat on the opposite side.

Energy Awareness Exercise

Do you have a sixth sense? You might without even realizing it. By *sixth sense* we do not mean some sort of advanced psychic ability, but rather the ability to sense energy. Following these exercises will help to develop your ability to feel energy, while also helping to calm and focus your mind.

FEELING ENERGY

Ki energy cannot be seen, but it can be felt. This exercise will help you learn to sense its presence. It requires deep, relaxed concentration, the perfect remedy for stressed-out brains. You should be as relaxed as possible before attempting this exercise, so stretch your body before you begin. At first, the feeling might be very subtle. Do your best to clear your mind and focus on that sensation. Keep practicing this and soon you will find that the sensation grows stronger.

1. Sit comfortably on the floor or on a chair and straighten your back.
2. Place your hands on your knees, with your palms facing up, and close your eyes. Relax your body, especially your neck and shoulders. Relax your mind. Inhale deeply; let go of any remaining tension while exhaling. (Soft meditative music in the background may be helpful.)
3. Raise your hands slowly to chest level, with your palms facing each other but not touching. First concentrate on any sensation you may feel between your palms. At first, you may only feel the temperature of your hands.

4 Now create about 2 to 4 inches of space between your hands and concentrate fully on the space. Imagine that your shoulders, arms, wrists, and hands are floating in a vacuum, weightless.

5 Pull your hands apart and push them closer together again as you maintain your concentration. You may feel a tingling sensation, like that of electricity, a magnetic attraction pulling your hands toward each other or pushing them apart. You may even feel as if you were holding a soft cotton ball between your hands or moving slowly through warm water. All these feelings are manifestations of your energy flow.

6 When the sensation becomes more obvious, pull your hands farther apart or push them closer together. The sensation will not leave you; it will expand and become stronger.

7 Breathe in and out slowly and deeply 3 times.

8 Rub your hands together briskly until they are warm; then gently caress your eyes, face, neck, and chest.

ABDOMINAL BREATHING

Breathing properly is essential for stress management. When you were an infant, you did this very naturally; no one had to teach you how. But over the years, your body began to collect a lot of tension, and soon your breath became shallow and incomplete. This is very unfortunate for your brain because it thrives on oxygen from your blood. Practice this exercise to learn how to breathe like a baby again.

1. Lie down on your back on a hard and warm surface.
2. Squeeze your legs tightly together and then completely relax them. They will part naturally, about the width of one foot. Your angle of your feet should be about 30 to 45 degrees from the floor.
3. Place your palms on your lower abdomen. Keep the elbows resting comfortably on the floor. If your elbows lift off the floor, allow the hands to slide down the sides of the abdomen until elbows rest on the floor.
4. Relax your body completely, especially the upper body, chest, and shoulders.

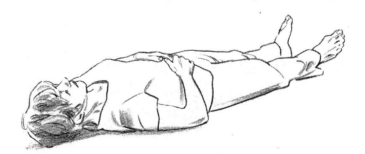

⑤ Curl your tailbone gently up, letting the lower back touch the floor as much as possible. As your tailbone tucks in, imagine creating a bowl in your lower abdomen to collect energy, trying your best not to tense your legs in order to do so. You will automatically feel slight tension in your lower abdomen.

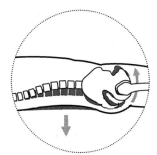

⑥ Close your eyes and focus on the energy flow inside your body. Breathe deep down to the lower abdomen.

CHAPTER 2

Your Versatile Brain

Learn young, learn fair; learn old, learn more.
Scottish proverb

In this chapter, we will discuss Brain Versatilizing, the process of creating new neural connections in the brain, which allows you to make your brain more flexible and to overcome resistance to changing negative habits.

In his book *The Memory Prescription*, Dr. Gary Small, director of the UCLA Center on Aging, writes, "Research has shown that it first takes a healthy and agile brain to motivate us to treat our bodies right and achieve our highest quality longevity throughout each phase of life."

We could not agree more. Health and vitality begin with the brain because this organ is where everything begins. Walking, picking up a child, kicking a soccer ball, stirring cookie batter in, and furling the sails on a boat at sea all begin the same way: a stimulus stirs an electrical signal between various areas of the brain that are related to the part of the body that is involved. Within milliseconds, those impulses travel from the brain, along the spinal cord, and into the branched nerves that control the arm we want to raise or the leg ready to be lifted into a conga-line kick. Voila—the movement happens. But it all begins in the cranium.

One of the more toxic ideas spread by modern culture is that the brain is static from birth to death. The conventional conception of the brain is that it grows in childhood and perhaps early adulthood, but at some point it begins to shed brain cells and neural connections begin to die, and this process is inevitable and irreversible. That may explain the deep dread with which many people regard aging: They assume that in their later years they will plummet into forgetfulness, senility, and finally the loss of identity. It is a fate that many of us fear more than the certainty of death: the possibility of mental decay.

However, as cutting-edge brain science is showing us, such decay is, for the most part, optional. It can be staved off or minimized with the proper actions. Most of us have been fortunate enough to know some person in his or her nineties, or even beyond, who is cognitively sharp, funny, and has the intellectual faculties of someone twenty years his or her junior. And when we speak to such wonderful seniors, whether as research scientists or as curious fellow human beings, we tend to hear the same stories. They have remained active and interested in many subjects throughout their lives. They read and play games. They have used the liberty of retirement to learn a new language or a new musical instrument. They are curious about science, religion, politics, and culture. They have kept their minds and brains churning and humming, and as a result they have athletic minds. So it is possible, if you are willing to adopt a brain-friendly way of life, to defy the ugly picture of brain deterioration.

Your Brain Is Never Too Old to Adapt

Science is a human enterprise, so it is as susceptible to bias and accepted beliefs as any other area of knowledge. For years, brain researchers accepted the conventional wisdom about brain function: It couldn't be improved. You had the brain you had developed in childhood and at some point in later life it started to decline. Unlike exercising your muscles and joints, they thought that no way existed to improve your brain's fitness. Even as recently as the late 1990s, this was dogma, unquestioned by medical science, including gerontologists dealing with diseases such as Alzheimer's.

But does that really make sense? After all, your brain exists in a kind of dual state: it creates and focuses your mental life, but it is also part of your physical being. Should it be the only area of your body that is unaffected by the beneficial effects of exercise, diet, meditation, and emotional fitness? Fortunately, the answer to that question is no. The brain, far from being the inert information processor that mainstream science considered it to be a few decades ago, is a dynamic, fluid system that is infinitely adaptable if you make a consistent effort. The various centers of the brain are interwoven with a galaxy of intricate neural fibers, trillions of neurons forming hundreds of trillions of connections. This tremendously complex system is designed to receive and send signals, so it is only sensible to conclude that it is designed to adapt to the strength and consistency of those signals. It turns out that this is true, and this is one of the most exciting advances in our knowledge of the brain. Your brain possesses a remarkable property known as neuroplasticity.

The basic meaning of neuroplasticity is that like a muscle, the physical brain responds to consistent, rigorous stimuli in a way that does not simply grow new neural connections, but actually changes the structure of the brain in order to more efficiently use the incoming signals. This means that your brain is never too old to grow and adapt to new tasks and challenges. In fact, it has great versatility.

An example can been seen in the brains of fast readers. In the brains of some people who read and absorb written information at high speed, time produces a change in the brain such that the pathways from the centers that process optical information to the centers of higher thinking become denser with neural connections, a sort of mental superhighway to allow the quickly acquired information to pass through the brain more quickly. Researchers have found similar changes in the brains of athletes and craftspeople.

Use It Or Lose Everything

If you spent years training your thoughts with mental challenges and demanding tasks, such as learning Greek or playing the saxophone, is it not likely that your brain would be more supple, responsive, and sharp? Clearly, we can train our brains like an athlete trains his or her body. The brain is unique as an organ that can be refined through our attention to it. That is the potential we find in neuroplasticity.

Based on the Bronx Aging Study, published in the *New England Journal of Medicine* in 2003, people with high IQs and more education have a lower risk of developing dementia as they get older. This may be because such people are more likely to engage in brain-intensive activities, or because they have more neural connections through genetic inheritance, or both. Either way, an active intellect appears to have more healthy neurons in reserve to be used when natural brain degeneration kills off some brain cells. This confirms the "use it or lose it" idea of brain health. Just as with any other part of your body, if you do not keep your brain active, its abilities will decline dramatically.

But we don't believe that "use it or lose it" really captures the importance of keeping the brain active and demanding increasingly rigorous work from it all your life. A more accurate way to phrase the statement would be "Use it or lose everything." As you age, your brain will decline in some ways. That is normal and is part of our evolutionary heritage; there is nothing you can do to avoid it entirely. But with so much of your brain matter underutilized, it is within your power to transform your brain through disciplined thought and action so that as you age you have reserves of brainpower to replace what you lose because of aging, stress, and the environment.

The Specter of Alzheimer's

We cannot speak realistically about the aging brain without addressing the frightening prospect of Alzheimer's disease. Alzheimer's is just one form of dementia, a disorder that can also be caused by diseases like Parkinson's or

Huntington's. Alzheimer's is most feared because of its terrible symptoms: confusion, language difficulty, memory problems, paranoia, and delusions. It is essentially a disease that robs you of selfhood.

In recent years, neuroscientists have discovered the likely cause of this condition: deposits of a protein called amyloid slowly build up in the brain over time and strangle healthy nerve fibers, destroying their neural connections. These plaques tend to concentrate their attack in the area known as the hippocampus, a region deep in the brain that, as we mentioned when we discussed exercise, is involved in memory. As the plaques spread, they disrupt central nervous system functioning in the brain, slowly destroying the areas of the brain responsible for memory and personality.

This living death is a source of terror for many older Americans. Many people over fifty begin to experience great anxiety every time they forget where they left their car keys. Some impairment of memory is normal as we age; it doesn't mean you have Alzheimer's. But the shadow of this awful disease stretches over seniors' lives like a shroud. For the most part, treatments for the disease slow its progression but accomplish little else. Stem-cell therapies show promise but are not available yet. People do not want to imagine themselves helpless and hopeless, unable to recognize loved ones. Fortunately, there is much we can all do to stave off such a fate.

The answer really comes down to one peice of advice: always seek new experiences. Novelty is one of the fountains of youth for the brain. Here we will return to a physical exercise metaphor. When you begin a workout regimen, at first you may find it difficult and your muscles become stiff, as if your body is shocked by the sudden increase in workload. But over time your body becomes accustomed to the greater cardiovascular work. Your metabolism increases to match your new workload. Exercise is no longer a shock. You reach a plateau. Only by introducing new elements into your workout can you expect to see continued results.

It is the same for the brain. When you engage in the same activities day after day, your neural pathways become very solid. There is no reason for new connections to form—why should they? Your brain has all the connections it needs to handle the demands you put on it. But when you demand more of your brain, when you start doing crossword puzzles, reading books in genres you have never read before, or engaging in lively political debates that challenge your preconceptions, you surprise your brain with new information, which is like adding a new element to a workout. The brain does not have the "wiring" to process these new questions and stimuli, so it is forced to forge new connections. Out come the neurological road crews to lay new electrical cables from one area of the cerebral cortex to another. Fresh nerve connections spark with electrochemical messages. Your brain activity increases. This is the only secret that matters: the secret of having a more youthful, agile mind into your eighties and nineties. Just challenge your brain in new ways every day.

Ask Your Brain

Your brain possesses infinite creativity, but most of us do not ask enough of our brains. Unless our brains are forced to find an answer to a new question, they are lazy. The brain uses only previously acquired information to meet the tasks of daily life. But when you ask your brain for something new, you put it into high gear. Your brain seeks out new information and links ideas and possibilities together in a complex web of informational elements that are the foundation of creativity and innovation. Asking your brain to engage in new tasks is the key to boosting its performance as you age.

Think about great human inventions: the airplane, the computer, the technology that made it possible to go to the moon. All of these began with simple questions: "Is it possible to do this? How can I do it?" Once you ask your brain questions, this marvelous organ begins searching for sources of answers. Your awareness expands as your brain seeks data and ideas through endless pathways: books, newspapers, the Internet, conversations with friends, daydreaming, your past experiences, and more. Everything in your world becomes a possible source of answers to your questions. What's more, your brain not only takes in information related to your question but also remembers chance encounters with information that might be of interest to you at a later time, so one inquiry might spawn a dozen later investigations into subjects from cosmology to cabernet.

You can see again how intention shapes your brain's functioning. When you ask your brain hard questions and trust it to bring you the answers, you expand your mental world. Your brain responds to the demands as your body does to a workout. Our brains are machines of inquiry and foray into the unknown. Have you ever wondered why humans seem so obsessed with discovery? Why for centuries have we sailed dangerous seas, trekked through pathless jungles in search of new species, and risked our lives descending into lightless caverns where no one has gone before? It's because we are wired to search and discover the new. Our brains demand it. To keep them truly alive, we must demand much of them.

Get Out Your Puzzle Book

Happily, you can reduce your risk of age-related dementia by doing some very simple, pleasurable things. Any activity that forces your brain to figure things out will help lower your chances of developing some form of dementia by making your brain generate new nerve cells. Dancing, which asks you to concentrate on music while moving your feet, results in a seventy-five percent reduction in Alzheimer's risk, according to a study cited in *U.S. News & World Report*. Many of the other activities that benefit the brain are surprisingly common: knitting, gardening, traveling, for example. If it forces your brain to make choices, coordinate your movements, or calculate strategies, it's helping your brain to remain healthy. The important thing is to do a wide variety of activities that stimulate various parts of your brain.

Some of the best options are the ones that really put your brain into high gear: reading new books, playing chess, doing tough crossword puzzles, learning to play a musical instrument, learning a foreign language, or learning a new skill such as sailing or carpentry. These are all great sources of brain benefit. Just developing the independent hand motion needed to play the piano proficiently rewires your brain in many ways, to say nothing of the gymnastics your brain goes through in learning the diatonic musical scale and remembering the difference between sharps and flats.

All this information supports the idea that older people should never truly retire if they want to retain mental and physical wellness into advanced age. It is one thing to leave your job; most of us want the freedom to control our time. But when you compare men and women in their seventies who remain active and seek challenges after ending their working life with, on the other hand, those who sit on the porch and rock, the difference is very clear. If you want to keep your brain and mind vital into your senior years, start a business, volunteer, or take up new hobbies, sports, and passions. If you want to see your mind wither and sputter and possibly rob you of your identity, retire from work and become a passive observer of life, stuck in your routine. The better choice is obvious.

The Rewards of Age

Of course, science is also showing us that age is more than a series of brain breakdowns that can be prevented only through diligent work and advanced cognition. Time also brings subtle yet meaningful positive changes to the brain, acquired through years of experience, that add to the quality of life. Dr. Gene Cohen, founding director of the Center on Aging, Health, and Humanities at George Washington University Medical Center, has discovered that the changes that come with aging actually make adults more able, as he writes, to "fulfill our own dreams."

Cohen found that though neurons lose processing speed as they age, they also have learned far more than young brains. This learning is represented physically in the dense maze of neural connections to be seen in an older brain. Cohen writes, "Magnified tremendously, the brain of a mentally active fifty-year-old looks like a dense forest of interlocking branches, and this density reflects both deeper knowledge and better judgment. That's why age is such an advantage in fields like editing, law, medicine, coaching, and management. There is no substitute for acquired learning."

You could call that the acquisition of wisdom. Cohen points out that with age our brains become in some ways less rigid and more adaptable, so that left-brained linear thinking and right-brained creativity are not as separate as they once were. Older people tend to use both sides of their brains more to solve problems, and are better at merging intuition with hard data to arrive at a conclusion. There is a reason why most CEOs are over fifty. They trust their gut but also rely on their logic for confirmation.

In addition, research has shown that older adults' brains show more emotional equanimity. The primitive part of the brain that brings out the fear response toward anything unknown becomes more dormant and positive feelings tend to replace negative attitudes. This is doubtless the source of emotional maturity, and it is related to one of the greatest rewards of the later years: deeper, more compelling personal relationships.

Studies show that people with strong social networks in the last one-third of life live longer, experience fewer health problems, and feel a greater sense of well-being than those who do not. Being with others is great for your health and your brain. One of the reasons for this is the damaging effect that stress, depression, and social isolation have on the brain. Chronic stress produces elevated levels of the hormone cortisol, which actually shrinks the memory centers in the brain and kills memory neurons. On the other hand, a recent UCLA study showed that when women of any age get together they produce more of the hormone oxycontin, which creates feelings of bonding and belonging. So deep, satisfying relationships—with circles of friends who go back decades, with fellow members of spiritually oriented centers and activist organizations, or with family members—are magic for alleviating stress and creating feelings of pleasure that bathe your brain in health.

Brain Versatilizing

The second step of BEST, Brain Versatilizing, is a process designed to help you develop a flexible and vibrant brain faster and more effectively than crossword puzzles and cross-stitching.

Brain Versatilizing is about challenging your brain to master new tasks and to become more adaptable and flexible. Through this practice, you will find yourself freed from rigid habits and modes of thinking and you will become more open to new information. Your brain will become a fluid instrument responsive to your commands. One of the greatest benefits of this is that you can break destructive habits such as smoking, losing your temper, or eating unhealthy foods. Habits are difficult to break because they become hard-wired into the brain in those deeply furrowed pathways we mentioned earlier. But in Brain Versatilizing you break up those pathways and bypass them with new ones. At advanced levels, you can actually change deeply ingrained biases and prejudices to develop a more open mind. What a gift! You will find that your cognitive experience is expanded and that learning new tasks becomes almost automatic. Your awareness will become wider as you activate areas of your brain that have been largely quiescent for years. We call this expanding the window of consciousness.

GRAY MATTERS:
MORE THINGS YOU CAN DO
FOR YOUR BRAIN

• PAY ATTENTION TO DETAIL

Look closer at the subtleties in things and people—the shadings and brushwork in two paintings, the fruit flavors in fine wine, or the body language of two people speaking on the other side of the room. Paying attention to minute detail is a spectacular workout for the brain.

• TRAVEL

Unfamiliar places and situations may make you uncomfortable, but that is the point. Dealing with unfamiliar customs, trying to speak the local dialect, and learning about new cultural wonders all earn you major brownie points from your cortex.

• BREAK YOUR ROUTINE

Stop doing things by rote. If you have been following a daily schedule for twenty years,

break it. This can be as easy as changing the order of the body parts you wash while you are in the shower.

• MEET SMART FOLKS

Talk to smart people–really talk to them. Engage in conversation that challenges your political or religious views and forces you to see other people's points of view. Ask questions, debate issues. Trading ideas forces your mind to ask questions, and that is always good.

• GET SHIFTY

No joke. University of Toledo researchers found that if you move your eyes back and forth for twenty seconds, like a pickpocket looking for his next victim, you stimulate the frontal lobes of your brain, which are responsible for memory. The researchers call it visual ping-pong. We call it effective.

Brain Balance Exercises

These exercises call on both sides of the brain to work together. Our tendency at all ages is to favor one side of the body, which neglects the use of one side of the brain. These exercises will challenge you to use the non-dominant side of your brain. Through them, you will develop new neurological connections that can be used for other mental tasks, such as memory recall and the learning process.

TRIANGLE CIRCLE SQUARE

When doing two tasks simultaneously, you challenge various parts of your brain to work together.

❶ In the air, draw a circle with your left hand and a triangle with your right, drawing the shapes continuously with both hands at the same time.

❷ Next, switch hands—draw a triangle with your left hand and draw a reverse circle with your right.

❸ Alternate hands and repeat the above. When you become proficient at drawing a circle and triangle, try drawing a square and triangle.

TAP AND SWEEP

This is a little like the old children's game of patting your head and rubbing your stomach at the same time.

❶ Tap your right fist on your right chest while your left hand sweeps up and down on the left side.

❷ Now switch sides, so that your right hand is sweeping and your left fist is tapping.

❸ See how fast you can switch back and forth.

THUMB AND PINKIE

Follow this movement with your eyes for a good eye workout and a fun challenge for the brain.

❶ Make your hands into fists and extend your arms out in front of your chest. Look at your fingers.

❷ Point your left thumb and right pinkie to the left. Now point your right thumb and left pinkie to the right.

❸ Keep switching left and right. See how fast you can switch back and forth.

ALTERNATING-FINGER COUNT

This exercise increases brain quickness and is also a good stretching exercise for the fingers and hands.

1. Hold out your hands in front of your chest with your fingers extended.
2. Fold down your thumb on the right hand while leaving your left thumb fully extended.
3. Now also fold down the index finger and thumb on the right hand and the thumb on the left hand.
4. Continue to fold down one finger at a time till they are all folded down.
5. Then start again, counting backward, and repeat 4 or 5 times.

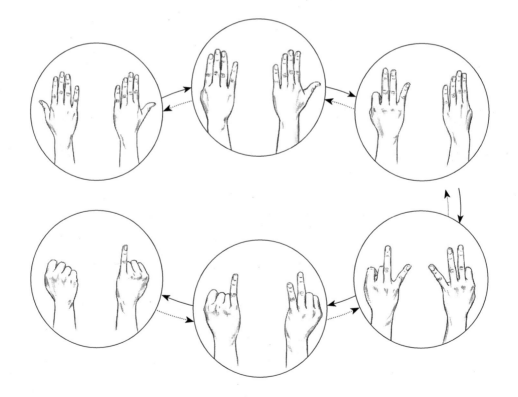

ROCK, PAPER, SCISSORS

This one will take a little time to master, so be patient! Try working on it while waiting in line or sitting in a waiting room as a way to develop your brain while passing the time.

1. Practice making the rock, paper, and scissors signs from the old decision-making game. Rock is a closed fist; paper is the hand flat, palm to the ground; scissors are two fingers extended. Practice with each hand until the motions feel natural.

2. Now make signs with both hands, showing the sign that cancels the right hand on the left hand.

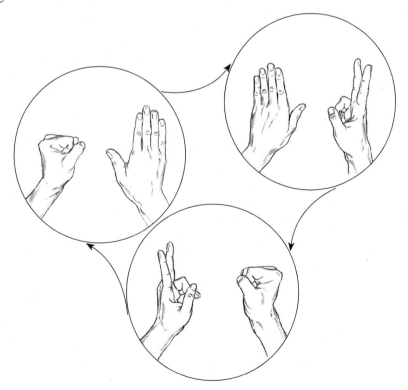

Body Balance Exercises

Since equilibrium is a brain skill that can decline quickly with age, it is important to practice these kinds of balancing exercises. If you deliberately work on your sense of balance, you can do a lot to slow, or even reverse, an age-related decline in equilibrium.

TRIUMPHANT TREE

To help keep your balance, focus just below your navel, inside your lower abdomen. This is the center point of your body, and thus is your center of gravity.

1. Stand with your feet together and your palms in the prayer position.
2. Slowly bring one foot up, placing the sole of your foot as high as you can on the inner thigh. Push your knee out to the side. (If this is difficult at first, place the foot lower on the leg.) Hold for 10 counts and then switch sides.

FEARLESS FLYER

This can be difficult, so start slowly and work up to the full posture.

1. Begin by standing with your feet together and your hands at your sides. Bend forward and place your hands on the floor. Your knees may be slightly bent.
2. Lift one leg up so that you are standing on one leg.
3. Slowly straighten the balancing leg as you slowly extend your arms out to the sides. Keep your body bent forward at a 90-degree angle, your arms out to your sides, and the other leg straight back. Hold for 10 counts.

ALTERNATE: Start with your hands on a table or chair, rather than on the floor.

Body-Brain Coordination Exercises

These exercises are similar to the Brain Balance exercises because they, too, involve coordination of left and right sides of the brain. Now the whole body gets in on the act, which requires the coordination of many parts of the brain at once. You will find that you have a dominant side of the body, just as you have a dominant hand. Use these to help reawaken the nondominant side of your brain for better coordination with your body.

OPPOSITE SHOULDER ROTATION EXERCISE

In addition to being a challenge for the brain, this exercise helps to open the shoulder joints.

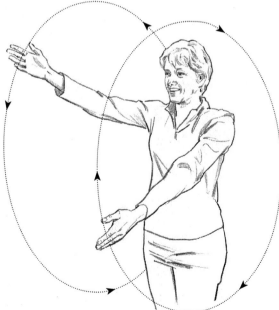

1. Stretch your arms straight ahead with your palms facing each other.
2. Rotate one arm clockwise while rotating the other counterclockwise.
3. Alternate directions and repeat.

QUICK CLAP

This is a great exercise to do in the morning to wake up your brain. The sound and the motion will stimulate your brain.

1. Clap once behind your head.
2. Clap once behind your back.
3. Clap once in front of your chest.
4. Repeat this sequence 10 or more times, as quickly as possible.

INFINITY COORDINATION EXERCISE

The infinity sign is used here because following its curved shapes helps to calm the mind while also promoting balance.

❶ Raise your thumb (pointing upward) to eye level, holding it at a point in between your eyes and away from your face. Gently bend your elbow so that your arm is relaxed. Trace the shape of the infinity sign (a sideways figure eight) with your thumb in the air, slowly and deliberately, with full concentration on the movement of your thumb. Hold your head still and follow your thumb with just your eyes. Repeat 3 to 5 times.

❷ Repeat with your left hand.

❸ You can also use both hands. Clasp your hands together with your thumbs crossing on top. Focus on the intersection of your thumbs and trace the shape of the infinity sign.

❹ If you work at a desk for a long time and often feel shoulder and neck stiffness, this is a good exercise to relieve tension and promote focus.

SPIRAL DANCE

This a great mind-body coordination exercise that also moves all the joints of the body.

❶ Place a small paper plate in your right hand. Hold it on your palm, without using your fingers. Spread your legs shoulder width apart and keep your left hand on your hip.

❷ Slowly bend the arm inward under the armpit, keeping the palm upward with the plate balanced on it. Swing the arm upward and to the front and over the head, creating a spiral motion. Move the hips as needed to facilitate the movement.

❸ Return to the original position, using a downward spiral motion. Repeat 5 to 10 times.

❹ Switch the paper plate to the left hand and begin the same spiraling movement on the left side. Repeat 5 to 10 times. Switch direction and repeat 5 to 10 times.

ADVANCED ALTERNATE PRACTICE: When the movement is fairly fluid on both sides, place paper plates on both hands and try completing the movement on both sides at the same time.

Continued on the next page ➜

Brain Flexibility Exercises

The following exercises are meant to help you learn to shift perspective easily and quickly. Normally, we have a lot of associations and preconceptions attached to just about anything we look at. Try these games and you start to think "out of the box."

RENAMING GAME

Look around the room and give new names to the things you see. Give each thing a name that normally belongs to something else. For example, rename the window "hamburger" and a pencil "horse." The only rule is that the new name cannot be associated with the object in any way. In other words, the window should not be named "door" and the pencil should not be named "pen." For more fun, play this with a friend. Take turns pointing out objects to name, and score a point for each correct (i.e. unrelated) name.

ALTERNATE USES

Take a look at the things in your home. You probably have a lot of tools and objects that perform specific functions—scissors for cutting, mallet for pounding, spoons for stirring, and so on. Now, take a look again and ask yourself what other tasks these objects might perform, aside from their intended use. For example, a compact disc might be used as a bookmark, a pastry cutter, or a Frisbee. A pair of nylon stockings might be used as a garlic holder, a cat toy, or a paint applicator. Play with a friend and see who can come up with the longest list for each object.

SHIFTING SENSES

When you take a walk, try shifting your focus from one sense to another. Our normal habit is to rely on the information given to the brain primarily through the eyes. This habit deprives your brain of the chance to develop and maintain your full range of senses throughout life.

So, instead of focusing only on visual information, try focusing on your other senses, one at a time. Try tuning in to your ears, recognizing and isolating as many distinct sounds as you can. Then do the same for your sense of touch—feel the breeze on your skin and the warmth of the sun penetrating your body. And continue with your sense of smell and even taste. Doing so will help to stimulate various parts of your brain and help you to keep your walks interesting and new.

RIGHTY LEFTY

What is more ingrained in the brain than handedness? To really challenge your brain, try doing everything with your nondominant hand, including writing. It may be difficult at first, but you will feel your capacity to use another part of your brain improving as your coordination improves.

CREATIVE SHAPES

Take a look at these shapes. How many different objects do you see? If you think three, look again. Think of things that the shapes remind you of— maybe the square is a TV and the circle is a penny. Draw on the following shapes to turn them into something new.

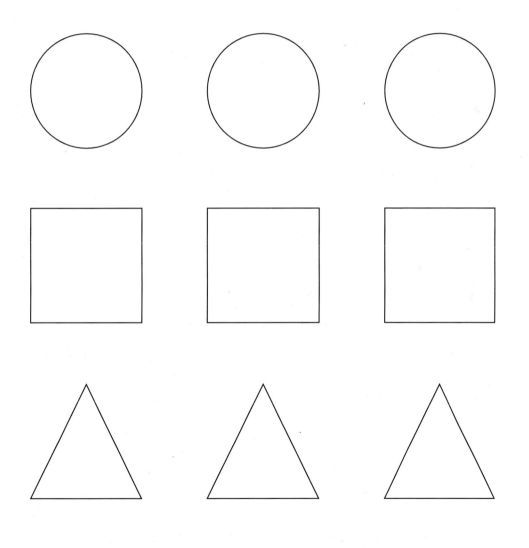

CHAPTER 3

Your Refreshed Brain

Emotions arise in the appetite and are brought into conformity with reason;
virtues are effects of reason achieving themselves in reasonable movements of the
appetites. Balanced emotions are virtue's effect, not its substance.
—Thomas Aquinas

The subject of this chapter is Brain Refreshing, the process of releasing negative emotional residue and letting go of past traumas. The goals: a more positive state of mind and greater, more productive control over your thought patterns.

Negative thought patterns are a major source of stress, and stress is the most common mental problem of our time. Hundreds of thousands of years ago, our hominid ancestors developed stress response systems that were designed to flood their bodies with powerful hormones in the face of a threat—an attacking bear or a dangerous deer hunt on the plains, for example. Those chemicals produced a wave of very useful physical and mental changes: more blood flowed to the heart and brain, the pulse raced, the skin temperature dropped, muscles tapped reserves of sugar energy, the brain sharpened and quickened. These responses were very important if you were a hunter-gatherer looking to outrace a wounded bison or fend off a hungry wolf. In this setting, the fight-or-flight response was very healthy.

However, attacking animals are rare in our modern world, and hunts on the plains are even rarer. Our mighty brains and our knack for technology have enabled us to become a race that uses its mind, not its muscle. We are farmers of information and hunters of data now. Rather than tracking prey in woodlands, we sit at desks in cubicles. Yet in terms of evolutionary time, we're just a few ticks of the clock from those savannah days, so our physical nature has not changed much. Back then, when the danger was over, our stress response was too. Our bodies relaxed to conserve energy. But today, under the pressures of work and traffic and debt and politics and war, our stress response is on overload. Many of us are "stressed out." Chronic, long-term stresses are our problem, and that fight-or-flight response does more harm than good. Those potent hormones are being dumped into our bodies constantly, which is not what nature intended.

As a result, our immune systems suffer. Our blood pressure spikes. We develop migraines, anxiety, and depression. In the short term, the stress response helps us. But chronic stress, hours every day, causes deterioration of both the body and the mind. And yet how easy it is to cleanse ourselves of such damaging effects! In chapter one you learned how to release tension from your body, but it is all for naught if you do not also learn how to release emotional tension from your mind. It is really a matter of choosing positive emotions to replace the negative, which is essentially what Brain Refreshing is all about.

One quick way to do this is to follow the old adage, "Laughter is the best medicine." Research shows that laughter reduces levels of at least four of the common stress hormones. A short, intense walk (it doesn't even have to be one mile long) can clear stress hormones from your bloodstream. And the simple act of taking a breath—something we do thousands of times each day without thought—can sweep away stress, relaxing the body and allowing it to rest and heal. But in today's world, even the simple act of proper breathing becomes difficult, as our bodies become full of stress-related tension. What's needed is deliberate attention to our breathing, emotions, and actions. Living consciously to shape one's emotions and attitudes is the next step in BEST.

Your Emotional Set Point

As we age, emotional health becomes more important than ever. After all, your emotional state is your constant companion throughout your life and should remain fairly consistent from your youth through your senior years. Assuming your brain is stable and well, the mental outlook you have at sixty-five can be healthier and more positive than the one you had at twenty-five, since you have the added benefit of life experience. Or it could be worse, if you allow yourself to fall into negative emotional habits. It's really up to you. One of the keys to this emotional wellness is balance between positive and negative, hope and realism, doubt and faith. You should be able to treasure memories of the past, while being able to let go completely of lingering pain and resentment.

However, this is not usually as easy as it sounds. As Verne Kallejian, Ph.D., writes, "Unfortunately, we have neither the philosophy nor the rituals in Western civilization to facilitate emotional health in the aging process. Very few life experiences prepare us to deal with the potential problems of aging. Nothing can easily replace the self-esteem of an important job or easily replace the friendships that are terminated by illness, death, moving to a new environment or other unexpected events."

As we age, the inevitable losses and changes of living can tilt our moods toward the negative. The death of a friend or loved one breeds loneliness and reminds us of our own mortality. Retirement, if the void is not filled with productive hobbies or volunteer work, can make us feel as if we have lost part of our identity. Failing health can cause anxiety or depression and contribute to one of the most harmful aspects of age: isolation. If a person lacks a proper sense of perspective or the cognitive tools to identify and change defeatist, dark thought patterns, it is easy to see how that person could, with age, become unpleasant and unhappy.

But as we age, destructive emotional patterns, resentment, and solitude are not inevitable. Current psychological theory holds that all of us possess "set points," life conditions that must be in place for our minds to feel a sense of well-being. You decide what conditions make up your set point and what emotions to associate with those conditions. For example, if your whole world has been work, you might associate retirement with uselessness and decay. In the remainder of this chapter, you will find specific exercises that will help you avoid these very dangerous pitfalls. And through the process of BEST, you will discover a sense of identity and purpose that will truly satisfy you.

Knowing and Cleansing Your Moods

At this level, BEST is all about three skills:

    a. Being fully aware of your emotions and moods
    b. Cleansing troubling, harmful emotions from your mind
    c. Developing the ability to change long-term temperament patterns

It is a myth that our emotions are beyond our control. Those who claim this are really saying, "I choose not to exercise control over my feelings." Often this attitude is born of a sense that negative emotions are just part of who we are—that feeling persistently angry or sad is something that just comes through the hard knocks of life. But how sensible is it to continue harboring such ideas when they wreak havoc on our bodies and our energies? The path of personal wisdom is to harness the brain's great powers of self-awareness—the watcher watching the watcher—to uncover the hidden patterns of mood and emotion that we bear within us and change the way we view the world. We have the power to change our set points, as it were. Have you ever wondered how some families living in poverty in the inner city or in a small village in the Third World can live with so much joy? It's because their set points are modest. They have each other, food to eat, a roof over their heads, and, often, their faith. That is all they need. What do you need to truly be happy and at peace with this life?

Let's differentiate between emotion and mood. Our marvelous brains recognize emotions from the time we are born. Feelings become hard-wired into our neural connections long before we can manage the complex dance of cognitive thought and language. Emotion is like weather; it is what we feel in the moment as we encounter the conditions and people in our lives. Mood is like climate; it lingers and engulfs us. Thus, we say, "He's in a bad mood." Moods are emotion made persistent and can go on for an hour, a day, or even develop into a life-long disposition. Sometimes, when a melancholy mood becomes dark and helpless and hopeless, and persists for a long time, it is called clinical depression.

Both emotion and mood create new pathways in the brain and release specific chemicals, from dopamine to epinephrine. But whereas emotions come and go, moods are a choice. Sometimes you cannot avoid situations that will bring forth anger, fear, irritation, or sadness. Life is filled with them and to avoid them is to avoid living. However, if you choose to have a positive view of the difficult things in life–if you possess strong self-esteem–those emotions do not affect you in the long run. You face them, deal with the situation that created them, and move on. However, moods do last and can shape your life in a healthful or dangerous way. If you hold on to insults, tragedies, or losses, or if you consider yourself responsible for them, you can breed dark, brooding, sullen moods that cause you nothing but misery. Friends stay away. Your health deteriorates. The world seems filled with no-good people and misfortune.

Brain Refreshing is your defense against such negative moods. Using breathing, meditation, and self-awareness exercises, it helps you catch yourself in the process of harboring negative emotions and helps you clear them from your brain. In this way, neural pathways that fuel troubling emotions are never built. The mind remains open to beauty and joy and a positive outlook. Remember, a world view is a choice!

The Persistence of Memory

Oliver Wendell Holmes said, "Memory is a net; one finds it full of fish when he takes it from the brook; but a dozen miles of water have run through it without sticking." This captures some sense of the elusive, ethereal quality of memory, yet memory is an important aspect of our identity. This is why so many people fear old age. They fear that they will inevitably have short-term memory loss, be unable to recall what they had for breakfast, or forget who they met the day before. But as Brain Education System Training shows, aging need not be that way.

First, understand that we know very little about the ways memory works. To be sure, we know the areas of the brain that are associated with short-term and long-term memory. There is also episodic memory (associated with past events), semantic memory (having to do with facts), spatial memory (allowing us to create a mental picture of what is around us), emotional memory (feelings and fears), and procedural memory (which helps us remember how to do something). The part of the brain known as the hippocampus and the various cortexes surrounding it are deeply involved in all types of memory, but many other areas of the brain work with memory as well. However, we really don't know what a memory is. Some scientists have thought it was an electrical trace left by an event in a specific part of the brain. But subsequent research has shown this trace theory to be mistaken.

The one thing we know for certain about memory is that it is central to our identities, and that a rich, active memory can be one of the great blessings of age. Wisdom, a source of wonderful stories, the images of people and places—these are all benefits of a strong memory. Unfortunately, as with our emotional habits, the loss of memory with aging has been thought to be something humans could not control. It was considered the luck of the genetic draw if someone's memeory remained intact into advanced old age. But as we are discovering every day, we have greater control over our lives than once thought. Memory, like mood, is a conscious act, and Brain Refreshing will help you build and maintain a strong memory.

Negative thought patterns spring from memories of unhappy events that you have clung to in your mind. They exert influence on your brain, leading to unproductive habits of thinking, preconceptions, even biases, all of which all have negative effects on health. Brain Refreshing helps you release the traumatic events of the past and clear your mind of burdensome memories. The result is deep emotional and spiritual healing—a renewal of your ability to look at life in a positive, healthful way. Gradually, you erase the negative neural pathways that were deeply dug into your brain like ruts in old roads. You create new highways to courage, inspiration, and serenity. This is very much a renaissance of the mind—a rebirth of the emotional freedom you experienced when you were a child.

If memories from the past do not haunt you, then perhaps the thought of losing your short term memory does. This is indeed a brain skill that declines with age. However, studies have shown that older people greatly overestimate their short-term memory loss. When you are twenty, misplacing your keys is absentmindedness; when you are sixty, it is a "senior moment." On top of that, memory degradation may be a cultural phenomenon, as young people are becoming less adept with their memory skills than the youth of previous generations, presumably because of the influence of information-storage technology.

Although Brain Refreshing is not specifically about improving memory skill, it can help with memory. It has been clearly documented that stress and negative emotions can get in the way of learning and memory. Stress literally shrinks the hypothalamus, the part of your brain in charge of memory. By freeing yourself from negative emotions and habits, you will be opening your brain to receive and store new information, like throwing away old files in a filing cabinet to make room for new.

Your Mellow Old Brain

You've probably heard that some people, like old wine, mellow with age. As it turns out, this is true of all of us because of the way our brains age. Researchers have discovered that older people generally have better emotional control and a more positive outlook on life. They theorize that the human brain is designed to shift from a more aggressive, competitive mode in youth to a more cooperative mode in later life. In the past, this may have been biologically advantageous as older people, no longer of reproductive age, shifted their attention to support of their kin, which indirectly assured survival of their genetic information.

Brain scans have revealed that older people simply process emotions differently, which may account for the improvement in emotional control. In the older people, more areas of the brain are shown to be active during the experience of emotions, especially in response to negative emotional stimuli. This finding suggests that life experience may provide additional brain connections to help neutralize negative emotions more quickly.

Overall, older people are healthier mentally than younger people. Incidence of neurosis decreases, and older people are less likely to report feelings of despair and worthlessness.

That being said, mental health is not automatic for older people. In fact, depression is common and the occurrence of suicide is more common among older people than it is among middle-aged people, especially among older men. Just because the older brain is better equipped to deal with negative emotion does not mean it is immune to emotional difficulty. After all, there are many aspects of aging that are difficult to handle, including death of friends, one's own physical decline, and the sense of aimlessness that can accompany retirement. It is best to prepare yourself with a strategy for emotional well-being in order to make the most of your brain's natural wisdom as you age.

Growing Your Emotional Intelligence

With the Brain Refreshing techniques of BEST, you will begin to hone your emotional intelligence, a term coined by Charles Darwin in 1872 but popularized in 1995 by author and psychologist Daniel Goleman. Emotional intelligence—the ability to perceive, assess, and manage your own emotions, as well as to deal with those of others—is one of the most valuable skills of the mature individual. When we are adolescents, adult passions appear in our minds unbidden: sexual longings, risk taking, the desire to acquire expensive, beautiful things. But because our prefrontal cortex, the area of the brain that lets us make social judgments and develop foresight about the possible outcomes of our choices, does not mature until the age of about twenty-five, emotion and passion can overwhelm us when we are young. Many young people lack the emotional intelligence to understand or control their powerful emotions. Instead, they are often on autopilot, led by their hormones and desires.

As we age, too many of us, unfortunately, swing to the opposite extreme. Because of some trauma in life, we shut our emotions down and divorce ourselves from them out of fear. We live in terror of admitting to our emotions. But this is not living. Despite the Western emphasis on the intellect, ancient wisdom shows us that people are complete only when they are ruled by their emotions as well as their intellect—when their passions and their judgment are given equal weight. But many adults, especially as they age, become afraid of their feelings. This is why so many seniors seem shut off, deaf to love, exultation, and joy. They cannot face what they have left behind. We consider this a tragedy since the senior brain possesses the potential to be something quite the opposite.

Emotional intelligence is the ability to assess one's emotions as they occur, to understand why they are occurring, and to manage their effects in real time. This is a deep level of self-awareness that is accessible through Brain Refreshing. The human brain has an extraordinary ability to reflect on its own functioning, and people with strong emotional intelligence can identify pessimistic feelings as they occur and put them in the proper perspective. Imagine being able to perceive your feelings of irritation when speaking with a friend who taxes your patience, as if you were an outside observer. You still experience the feeling, but you have the presence of mind to know where it is coming from and remind yourself, "He doesn't really mean to be irritating; it's best to let that feeling go." This enables you to set aside such unhelpful emotions and retain your positive outlook toward other people.

Emotional intelligence is a very important life skill, and the later years of life are a great time for its expression. When you are able to face painful memories and let them wash out of your mind, you see the power that you once granted those memories. You discover that they have no power of their own and had only the power that you gave them. You are now in control of what triggers your emotions; they are not in control of you. You could say that you are achieving the highest potential of your emotional brain. Your mind becomes free to pursue its higher purposes—love, compassion, creativity, health, discovery, healing others.

Older people with strong emotional intelligence can and should serve as "emotional mentors" to younger people who are struggling to let go of their own emotional baggage. Clearer perspective on emotion also lends older people the vision to become leaders in the community, where decisions must be made based not only on one's gut feelings, but on everyone's demonstrated needs. Best of all, this kind of emotional awareness can renew lifelong relationships by allowing you to let go of meaningless grudges and focus on the positive, affirming traits of the people in your life.

Change Your "Longitude"

Put together *longevity* and *attitude* and you get *longitude*. This kind of longitude may help you become oriented in life, but we are not talking about the lines on a map that let you know how far east or west of some point you are. We are talking about the territory defined by your mental approach to life. When you refresh your brain and break the hold that negative memories have over your emotions, you change your longitude. Finding your longitude is about locating what is most imporatnt to you in life and then observing where you are in relation to those things. In other words, you focus on what you value most, not on past disappointments. By choosing to let go of past pain and view life with a more positive, uplifting, joyful attitude, you will increase your longevity. Equally important, you will increase your enjoyment of life. Quantity and quality—for what more could anyone ask?

There are many randomized, controlled studies proving the link between a positive mental state and better health and longer life. One of the most thorough is a study that was published in 2002 in the *Journal of Personality and Social Psychology*. The work, completed at Yale University, tracked hundreds of adults over fifty for 23 years. It found that "those who had a positive attitude towards aging lived roughly seven and a half years longer than participants who were dreading reaching their twilight years. The apparent life-extending benefits of a positive attitude remained even after the researchers accounted for other factors that can influence longevity, such as health, gender, and socio-economic status."

A positive attitude had an even greater effect on health and long life than maintaining low cholesterol or normal blood pressure. Of course, it may be that people with a positive outlook are more likely to take care of their health and suffer less from stress. But we think there is more to it than that. The mind has an extraordinary ability to affect the body, so why should it be any surprise that a diseased mind, riddled by anger, regret, fear, and resentment, should bring on the same disease in the body? In any case, the effects of improving your "longitude" are clear. As you can see, doing so is a conscious choice anyone can make at any time. It is never too late. Seeing the world with greater hope and kindness improves your health, clears your mind, frees your creative brain, and improves the overall quality of your life.

What Is Brain Refreshing?

Brain Refreshing is a holistic blend of breathing techniques, meditation, and energy balancing that is designed to give your brain an intense cleansing of negative memories and to encourage stronger emotional self-awareness. Deep breathing is renowned for its power to induce profound relaxation and help bring the mind into deeper and deeper states of meditation. Most of us breathe shallowly all day long, but deep, intentional breathing oxygenates the brain and enhances feelings of well-being.

Meditation, as we have already discussed, has been shown to offer many benefits to the brain. Research using modern imaging technology has shown that even novices who spent weeks in meditation training experienced a strong shift in their brain activity to the part of the brain associated with positive emotions, as well as a more robust immune-system response. While practiced as part of many Asian spiritual traditions, meditation is not strictly religious, but rather an ancient, proven method of relaxing the body, opening the mind, and deepening feelings of connectedness and peace. Learning the skills of meditation will enhance your life in many ways.

SIMPLE WAYS TO ADJUST YOUR "LONGITUDE"

• PRACTICE RANDOM KINDNESS

Go out of your way to lend a hand or say something nice to someone without being asked. Put a quarter in a parking meter that's about to expire, help a woman with her groceries, give $20 to a homeless person you see daily. You will be surprised by how good helping someone makes you feel.

• LOOK FOR BEAUTY AROUND YOU

Stopping to find the beauty around you is a sure way to erase those frown lines from your forehead. When you feel a negative mood coming on, look around you. Notice the flowers, the shapes of the clouds, the texture of a piece of pottery, the plumage of a bird. Anything can be beautiful when you look at it with a sense of wonder and gratitude.

• TALK WITH PEOPLE

Isolation kills. Company saves. One of the reasons Okinawans have one of the longest life spans in the world is that they usually belong to a *moai*, a mutual support network of family and friends that goes back decades. Make a point of talking to someone close to you every day. If you can, have lunch or share a walk. Few things make you feel more connected than shared history.

• LIVE IN THE MOMENT

We all rush around at such great speed that we are always looking ahead. What's next? What's on my list? At least once each day, stop and be in the moment, using all your senses: sight, hearing, taste, smell, touch. It might be in the produce section at the grocery store—it doesn't matter. Stop and just be. Appreciate being where you are, doing what you are doing. Ask yourself what is memorable about this moment.

• COUNT YOUR BLESSINGS

When all else fails and you feel a foul mood overtaking you like a storm cloud, take a moment and reflect on how lucky you truly are. You are alive. You have endless potential and possibilities. Things are never as bad as they seem. Think of ten things for which you are truly thankful.

This work conditions the energy centers in the human body. In Brain Refreshing, you will learn to heal and awaken your internal energy sources and open the flow of vital energy to your entire body. Through this training, you will create a more balanced energy system in your body and mind, which brings greater health and contentment. Through these practices, you will experience a sloughing off of timeworn attitudes, grudges, and negative patterns of thinking, and an intense renewal of your mind.

The intention of Brain Refreshing is not only to release and clear away negative emotional memories and non-useful information, but also to gain mastery over your emotions and to realize that happiness can be created anytime and anywhere through action. This whole process will empower you to channel new energies to your brain and enjoy the new clarity and joy life brings you.

Self-Reflection Exercises

Researchers have found that imagining something stimulates the brain in ways very similar to actually experiencing it. That is why it is important to keep very positive, supportive images in your mind. Negativity can quickly become a habit if you focus on negative experiences. Use these exercises to become aware of your emotional habits.

EMOTIONAL INVENTORY

It is important to recognize what memories are still with you, replicating emotions long after the events have passed. Take a look at the following emotions and identify particular memories that you associate with each.

Happiness	
Sadness	
Anger	
Fear	
Joy	
Frustration	
Love	
Serenity	

YOUR HAPPIEST MOMENTS

You may have the habit of dwelling on mistakes of the past or worries about the future. Break that habit by taking some time to revisit happy times in your life. Before you begin, sit down or lay down, relaxing your body completely. Close your eyes and recall in the most vivid detail possible times that you felt great joy and comfort. Think of childhood and adult moments alike. Relive every aspect of the experience as if it were happening right now. Choose some of your happiest memories and use them to shift your brain back to positive mode whenever you find yourself losing your positive point of view.

AGE-ITUDE INVENTORY

Even if you have had a very positive mindset throughout your life, negative thinking can arise as you age if your associations with aging are negative. Take some time to make a list of all the things you associate with aging. Put positive attributes in one list and negative attributes in another. Is one list longer than the other? Can "negative" items be put in the other list if you see them from a different angle? As you read through the rest of the book, see if you can continue to add items to the list of positive attributes.

Emotional Release Prep

These exercises will help you get ready for the process of releasing. You can also use them when you begin to feel negative emotions beginning to rise. They will help to make the process of releasing more effective and relaxed.

HEAD TAPPING

To further release tension from your head and face, try tapping them with your fingertips. This exercise will also increase blood flow to the skin, so it is a good beauty tip, too! Just curl your fingers and begin tapping firmly all over your face and head. Make sure you tap all over your head, especially your temples and crown. On your face, target places that are holding tension, such as the jaw, cheekbones, and around the eye sockets.

FACIAL RELEASE

A great deal of tension can be held in the face, and it often becomes habitual. Try this and you will find it very hard not to smile.

1. Squeeze all your face muscles; close your eyes, nose, and mouth tightly. Hold for about 5 counts.
2. Open your eyes, nostrils, and mouth as wide as you can.
3. Breathe in, and as you return your face to normal, exhale.
4. Repeat this sequence at least 3 times.

LYING VIBRATION

Have you ever seen a little kid lie down on the floor and flail his arms and legs when upset? We don't recommend this as a way of dealing with your boss, but it does make energetic sense. Use it to shake loose your emotions.

1. Lie comfortably on the floor.
2. Lift your arms and legs into the air and begin to shake them lightly.
3. Counting slowly to 10, shake harder and harder until you reach the count of 10.
4. Drop you arms and legs gently to the floor. Breathe deeply and relax.

TOE TAPPING

This exercise is great for releasing emotional tension from the body, bringing energy away from your head to your lower body. Also, it is a great cure for insomnia, when your head is full of worries.

1. Lie on your back with your feet and legs together.
2. Place your hands on the floor with your palms on the ground. Flex your feet back and keep your heels close together.

❸ Tap your big toes together, then open your feet so that your little toes tap the floor. Repeat as rapidly as you can.

❹ Start with 100 repetitions and increase the number after more practice.

Emotional Release Exercises

Emotions are the primary reason we place limits on our brain. It is because of emotions that we tell ourselves, "I can't try that. I will only embarrass myself." Out of fear, we stop short of our dreams, and because of past hurts we close ourselves off to others. Fortunately, it is possible to relieve your mind of debilitating emotions, but you must first learn to let go of them.

LAUGHING EXERCISE

You already know that laughing is powerful medicine. But unfortunately you can't buy laughing pills at the pharmacy. You could go to a funny movie or meet with a funny friend, but why rely on them? You can laugh any time you want.

So try sitting down on the floor one day and laugh to your heart's content. You may ask, "But how can I laugh if there is nothing to laugh about?" Just try it. Just laugh as hard as you can. At first, it will seem awkward, but keep going. Flail your arms and pound the floor, busting up with laughter. Soon, you will feel like a kid again.

BRAIN BREATHING

Through this exercise, imagine hurting, negative emotions being replaced with bright, positive emotions.

1. Sit in a comfortable position and place your hands on your knees, with your eyes closed. Relax your body and mind by taking several deep breaths. Feel the stream of energy move from the top of your head, down to your chest and then to your lower abdomen.

2. Concentrate on the top of your head.

3. As you breathe in through your nose, imagine a stream of energy entering through the top of your head, circling around your head, and clearing your brain of negative emotional energy.

4. Breathe out through your mouth with a soft whooshing sound. Imagine stagnant, negative energy being expelled from your body.

5. Breathe in and out slowly as you imagine bright light entering and darkness moving out.

6. Breathe in and out 3 times and open your eyes.

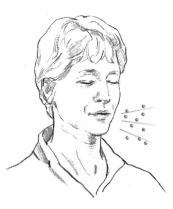

7. Rub your hands together until warm, and gently massage your head and face.

SMILING MEDITATION

The act of smiling produces positive changes in your brain. This exercise combines that fact with a relaxing meditative exercise.

1. Sit comfortably and shrug your shoulders up and down several times to relax.

2. Breathe in and out several times, massaging your face to release the tension in your facial muscles.

3. Breathe in, close your eyes gently, and breathe out while forming a slight smile. Breathe in and out deeply and naturally.

4. When breathing out, combine your exhale with a widening smile. Repeat this several times, focusing on the motion of the smile on your face as a light breath escapes through your lips like a gentle wind.

5. Slowly shift your consciousness to your brain and feel your brain become lighter and more refreshed when you breathe out with a smile.

Healing Guide

Human touch is one of the best methods of emotional healing. Sadly, touch is often discouraged socially in our culture. Using these healing techniques will be very beneficial for your brain, whether you are teaching them to others or are experiencing them yourself.

SHOULDER MASSAGE

The shoulders very commonly hold tension. Fortunately, they are also an easy place to give a quick massage to a friend.

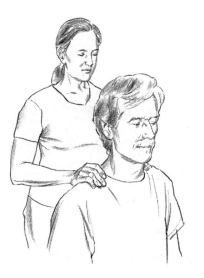

❶ Squeeze the trapezoid muscles, which extend from the neck to the shoulders, with the flat part of your hand, without pinching. Release and repeat several times, working your way up and down the muscle.

❷ Work your hands down the sides of the shoulders, squeezing and releasing.

❸ Use your thumb and palms to release tension around the shoulder blades.

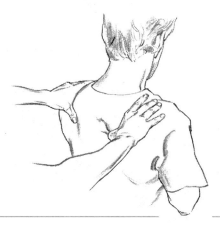

HAND MASSAGE

In reflexology, places on the hand are believed to be related to all the other parts of the body. So if you give a hand massage, it is the next best thing to a full-body massage.

❶ Squeeze the hand, moving from the wrist to the fingertips.

❷ Holding the palm open, push your thumbs firmly into the point where the wrist and palm meet. Work toward the center of your palm, pushing firmly with your thumbs.

❸ Gently pull and twist each finger between your own, working down to the fingertips.

FOOT MASSAGE

After a long day, nothing rejuvenates a person like a foot massage. If you do not have a partner, try giving one to yourself.

① Squeeze the foot from the ankle to the toes.

② Flex the foot in both directions and then rotate the ankle. Pull and fan out the foot.

③ Push your thumbs firmly into the foot at the indentation just below the ball of the foot. Massage in a circular direction.

④ Work in a line down the center of the foot.

ABDOMINAL HEALING

You may remember the comfort you felt as a child when your mother rubbed your tummy if you weren't feeling well. As an adult, you can give and receive the same kind of comfort.

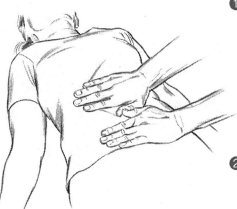

❶ Have the person lie down on the floor comfortably. Sit close to the person and place your hands on the abdomen above the navel. Focus on the warmth of your hands and the rhythm of the breath.

❷ With your hands slightly cupped, begin to rock the person gently back and forth.

❸ With the base of your palm, begin to work in a circular motion around the abdomen.

CHAPTER 4

Your Integrated Brain

Each material thing has its celestial side;
has its translation, through humanity, into the spiritual and necessary sphere,
where it plays a part as indestructible as any other.
—Ralph Waldo Emerson

Our discussion here concerns Brain Integration. This aspect of BEST works to reunite the diverse processing centers of the brain, reviving dormant connections between thought, emotion, and reasoning and helping you to discover your true self.

The human brain is the most complex structure we can imagine. Its billions of neurons interweave in countless neural connections, and it is a living, dynamic system. Millions of nerve cells die every day while more are created as a result of new experiences. Though we have made great leaps in our knowledge of the hormonal, electrical, and functional operation of this amazing organ, we are still light years away from understanding how the physical brain gives rise to self, awareness, and consciousness.

According to a 2006 study conducted at the Yale School of Medicine, the brain uses both digital and analog coding for communications across its expanse. Digital signals, the yes/no option that defines today's computers in everything from cars to video cameras, are very efficient and were thought to be enough for the brain to do its complicated work. Not so. It turns out that analog signals, which depend on changes in the voltage of the electrical impulses that drive our brains, are also involved. The result is a solution far more subtle and efficient than we ever expected. Our brains are full of surprises, as are we. Your brain gives you the potential to reinvent yourself at any age.

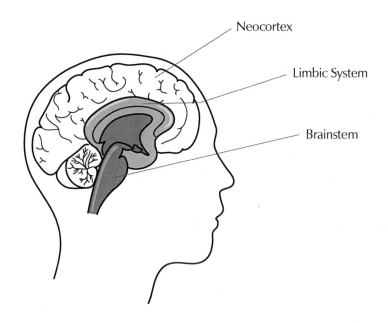

Three Layers of the Brain

Your Three-Level Brain

In a way, your brain is three brains layered together. It has three distinct parts that echo our evolutionary past. At the deepest level is the reptilian brain, or R-complex. This is the brain we inherited from our distant ancestors, long before there were human beings. This brain is home to our most primitive instincts: reproduction, movement, the fight-or-flight response, and territoriality. The reptilian brain tends to be very resistant to change.

Above the R-complex is the limbic system. The parts of this higher brain control learning and memory, the expression of emotions, and the linking of past events to strong emotions. So when you remember a traumatic breakup with a boyfriend or girlfriend many years ago and feel the anger or grief again, that is your limbic system in action. This center is also responsible for attachment and protective, loving emotions, so it might be called the source of our emotional intelligence.

Finally, at the top of the evolutionary ladder is the neocortex. This is the youngest and largest part of the brain, the seat of higher thinking, writing, and language, our ability to reason and analyze, and our power to anticipate the future.

These three brains perform their own specific functions, but they are also deeply interconnected, linking thought, emotion, memory, and action in complex ways that make us human. This network of nerves has the potential to make our brains agile and perceptive and our emotional lives rich and rewarding no matter how old we are. Yet often this potential is not reached, because the traumas or habits of decades damage the flow of energy between these brain centers.

Brain Integration heals the damage. This discipline makes it possible for you to more fully integrate your thoughts and your emotions and bring out your whole true personality. The result? A healthy body, enriched emotions, and blooming creativity—you become the person you have always aspired to become.

The Roadblocks of Age

Through the years, you've formed a sense of self, a way of identifying the person you are. Your work, your relationships, your family, your faith, your health—these are all parts of that mental self-portrait that you have labeled *Me*. But as the years pass, life can become less about stability and more about transition. Loved ones and friends pass away. You retire from a long career. Kids move out. You leave the home where you have lived for decades.

These changes can shake your sense of identity and leave you feeling rudderless, out of control. The finely tuned integration of your thoughts, emotions, and actions can fall away. Your thinking becomes muddled and outbursts of anger or periods of depression become more common. As you realize that some of the jarring transitions you're experiencing are permanent, it is tempting to think that your identity is lost. If you are not your work, your marriage, your healthy body, or your home, who are you?

This can be a difficult, challenging time of life. It is understandable to be frightened when we are faced with the dissolution of all that we think makes us who we are. But if you choose to adopt a BEST perspective, this can also be a time of tremendous potential for the future.

Reinventing Yourself

You are not simply your thoughts, habits, memories, emotional responses, triggers, and biases. That would be like saying a computer is merely a collection of microprocessors and disk drives. But a computer, properly assembled, becomes a tool for writing this book, sending people into space, or changing the world. So too are you not simply the sum of the three parts of your brain, but their combined potential. It is possible to view the transition periods of later life not as crises but as opportunities to redefine the person you are. Brain Integration fuels that redefinition.

Brain Integration unifies the disparate centers of your brain, restoring the flow of energy and renewing communication. The process allows you to let go of the sense of self that depended on aspects of your life that have changed, and empowers you to create a new identity based on today—your new pursuits, relationships, and passions.

Imagine being able to shed your outdated sense of self and to let go of the unwanted influence of other people and events. You become free to decide what parts of your new life will define you and to fully experience your emotions without fear. Brain Integration establishes new, robust connections between your three brain centers and the hemispheres of your brain—the linear and analytical left brain and the creative and intuitive right brain. You will be able to unleash your creativity, control your emotions, and approach situations from both a rational and intuitive perspective.

Instead of a brain fragmented by traumas during the aging process, you will find your lifetime of experiences and knowledge meshing like the parts of a wonderful machine, carrying you to new levels of insight, including:

- Expanded awareness of your environment
- A sense of the oneness of existence
- Greater self-awareness
- The development of new talents
- Deeper, more satisfying emotional relationships
- Greater wisdom

Older individuals who practice Brain Integration frequently find themselves attracted to new pastimes and activities, discovering new life purposes, and healing their relationships with friends and family. Who knows, you might discover a love for writing you never knew you had, decide to mentor a young scholar, or join a new circle of friends who are on the same life journey as you are. Brain Integration is challenging, but once you have completed the first three steps, you will be ready.

Go Deep

Brain Integrating is very self-reflective; it demands that you speak to yourself with total honesty. Building on your earlier BEST work, in which you learned to let go of previous pains and preconceptions, you will question your basic perceptions about yourself and about life.

You will ask fundamental questions about your Self, the conscious observer. As you silence your critical, self-doubting mind, you will begin to hear your brain speaking in an unfiltered way. This organ partakes of the larger truths of the spiritual world; it is your link to a greater, unified wisdom.

Once you are not trying to influence the flow of that wisdom by what you find socially, politically, or spiritually acceptable, you will see fresh truths. Not all of these truths will be comfortable. That's all right. Change is not always comfortable. But approaching it with courage is the key to happiness.

As we get older, we become more set in our ways. It may be that for years, without knowing why, you have voted for a particular political party, adhered to a certain religious path, or held a belief about a group of people without ever really knowing why. We tend to ignore facts that contradict our long-standing beliefs. This tendency is known as confirmation bias, and our brains are designed for it.

A 2004 study conducted at Emory University showed that during a period before the 2004 presidential contest between George W. Bush and John Kerry, thirty men, half of whom described themselves as "strong Republicans" and half of whom called themselves "strong Democrats" were asked to judge opposing statements by the candidates. MRIs showed that the part of the brain associated with reasoning was not active during this activity. The parts involved in emotions, conflict resolution, and making judgments about moral accountability were running the store. In other words, we believe what we want to believe.

The higher cognition enabled by Brain Integration frees you from this way of thinking. Instead of being under the control of unconscious brain processes, you control your mind's functioning. You are in the pilot's seat. You are in command. You consciously blend emotion, analysis, and experience to make the best decisions. After all, what's the use of having sixty, seventy, or eighty years of hard-earned wisdom and judgment if you can't use it to have the rewarding, generous, loving life you have always wanted?

Provocative Questions

Part of this process is asking yourself challenging questions, the kind most of us rarely take the time to ask or answer. The questions will be different for everyone, as will the answers, but here are some examples that should get you going in the right direction:

- What kind of person do I want to become?
- What do I want my later life to be like?
- What are my goals?
- What past pain am I ready to forget?
- Who do I need to forgive?
- What quality do I most want to develop in myself?

These are not easy questions. But your brain is equal to any task; after years of experience, you have the knowledge within you to answer such questions. The key is to trust yourself, not to shy away from what your deep self-exploration tells you. You have seen much and have deep insight. Trust your ancient wisdom. Congratulate yourself on having the ability and the courage to probe the subterranean depths of your consciousness.

Creating a New You

Asking such questions is only part of the process. The second part of Brain Integration is to craft a revitalized, refreshed identity from the knowledge you gain. You are not erasing the person you were; that man or woman still exists. All your past experiences exist as a source of your wisdom and judgment. But you are no longer trapped by your old identity, either. Instead, you're essentially reconstructing yourself, tearing a beloved house down to the foundation, saving the wood, stone, and glass, and erecting a new house with the same materials. You end up with a fresh, exciting new building that has the same foundation as before. You become a new incarnation of the person you have always been, with a new identity constructed from your values, beliefs, abilities, goals, and accomplishments, and the way you feel about yourself.

When you begin the sentence, "I am a person who..." you usually finish with a statement regarding what you hold dear (such as, justice, money, or family), what you can do (sing, run a marathon, speak Dutch), what you want in life (to be a teacher, to read Marcel Proust) or what you believe in (God, democracy). As you ask yourself questions, you will discover new values, beliefs, goals, and abilities that were hidden in the many layers of your mind. You will see some of your cherished values and beliefs in a new light, and they will be rearranged and reconsidered. You will have the construction materials you need to build a clearer, stronger, more joyous identity that reflects your vast potential.

"I Didn't Know I Could Do That!"

You've probably heard this old joke before:

A man goes to his doctor after being treated for a broken hand. "Tell me, Doc, will I be able to play the violin?"

The doctor examines the man's hand. "Yes, I think so."

"That's pretty cool. I could never play it before."

Have you ever had the desire to do something like play the piano, but been convinced you lacked the natural ability? That is latent ability—talents or skills you have within your subconscious but don't express in your normal life. We all possess such abilities, but most of us never discover them. The fragmentation of our brains and the endless stresses of daily life keep them hidden away.

One of the wonderful rewards of Brain Integration is that you will begin to discover your latent abilities. If you are at retirement age or beyond, this is especially gratifying. After all, you are at the age where old dogs aren't supposed to learn new tricks. Yet only by continually growing and learning do you keep brain and body young. How great, then, to find that you can play the violin, so to speak!

Each human brain contains the potential for hundreds of skills and talents, from speaking Italian to cooking like a chef in the finest Paris restaurant. What if you could tap into some of your hidden talents? What if you could, at age sixty or seventy, learn to read music and sing with a chior, or take up repairing and restoring classic motorcycles? How much delight would that bring to your life? Whatever you choose, make sure that it is something truly gratifying and fulfilling to you. Take the word *can't* out of your vocabulary. Remember that your brain has neuroplasticity, the ability to create neural connections in response to new experience. Discovering your latent abilities is a fantastic way to stimulate your brain to adapt and improve through the years.

A New Consciousness

When you have achieved Brain Integration, you will be more in charge of your brain. Instead of being a sideline observer of processes that go on by themselves, you will be more in command of what your brain does and how you respond. You will have what psychologists call metacognition. This means you are aware of your own mental operations—aware of the workings of your mind.

When you reach this state, everything changes. Even if you spent the first sixty years of your life being afraid of risk, you'll be able to see your fear coming on, stop it, analyze it, and choose to respond differently, all in the blink of an eye. That is power. That is true self-awareness: the power to command the choices you make. It will change your life.

Asking the Right Questions

In Brain Integration, much depends on the quality of the questions that you ask yourself. The depth and courage of your questioning will determine the usefulness of the answers that your mind brings to you. When you are contemplating this part of BEST, we suggest you begin your questioning process in some of these areas:

- Your relationships
- Your spiritual beliefs
- Your life goals
- Your sense of identity
- Your personal character
- Your questions about the meaning of life

Do not limit yourself to these, however. They are merely starting points if you have trouble focusing your mind. If you can, open your mind in relaxation and let it lead you where it wishes to take you.

Circuit Drawing

These simple drawing activities provide two valuable benefits. First, they increase hand-eye coordination. Second, they create a meditative rhythm that helps you soothe and calm your brain waves. Don't forget to switch hands to develop the nondominant side of the brain. These actives can be used for Brain Versatilizing activities as well. Begin with the infinity symbol on the next page, and then work up to more advanced figures.

1. Draw the figure on a sheet of paper. Preferably, use large paper so your whole arm can move, not just the wrist. Keep tracing the symbol for several minutes, until the movement is smooth and balanced.
2. After the image becomes relatively easy to draw, switch directions.
3. Now switch hands and try the same thing with your nondominant hand. Continue until the movement is smooth and relaxed. Also, try drawing them with your eyes closed.

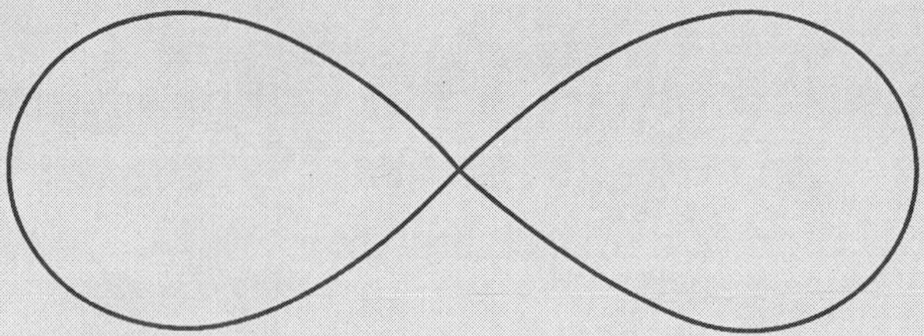

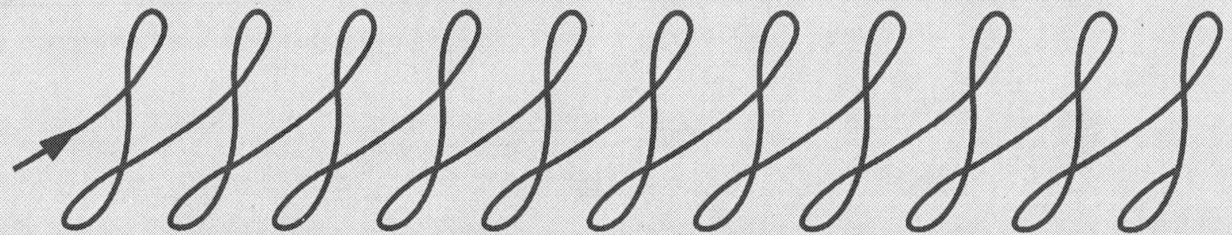

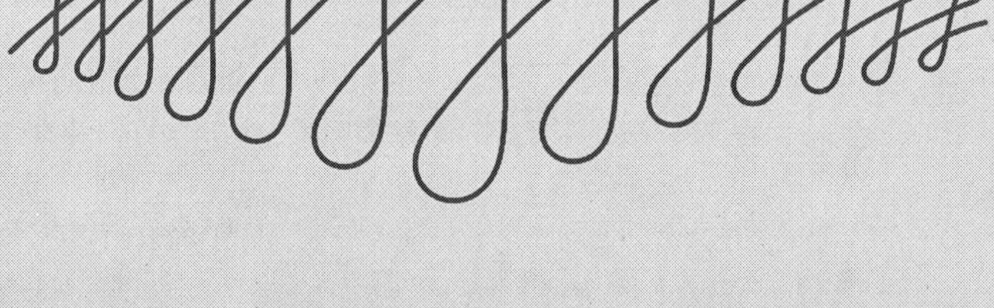

Brain Wave Vibration

We have a highly developed neocortex. It is so dominant that it sometimes leads to suppression of the limbic system and the brainstem. The best way to tone down the activity of the neocortex and maximize the effeciency of the brainstem is with a repetitive, continuous rhythm, as when you fall asleep to the monotonous hum of an air conditioner.

Brain Wave Vibration exercise uses repetitive rhythmic vibration to tone down the activities of the neocortex, activate the limbic system, and allow you to connect with the life energy that resides in your brainstem.

Brain Wave Vibration allows you to take initiative to ignite a vibrational reaction in your own body. There are not any set or predetermined patterns for self-vibration. You just let your body go along with the natural rhythm of life. If you like, play music with a strong, rythmical drum beat. Release any self-consciousness that interferes with giving free rein to your movements. Do not be upset when stray thoughts and emotions enter your mind. Just let them pass.

BRAIN WAVE VIBRATION—STANDING POSTURE

❶ Stand with your feet shoulder-width apart. Let your hands hang at your sides in total relaxation.

❷ Begin by slightly bouncing your knees up and down. Let this movement expand through your whole body, until every part of your body is shaking up and down in unison.

❸ Gradually let the natural vibration of your body take over. Let your body create its own rhythm. Feel everything in your body, including your lips, tongue, eyes, and skin. Your breath will naturally become synchronized with your movements.

❹ As you continue to vibrate, imagine your brainstem, located at the base of the skull, glowing with energy. Imagine this energy slowly spreading up into your brain, down your spine, and out through your nervous system until every cell of your body is bathed in energy.

❺ Your conscious awareness will disappear as you become aware of only the vibration. Once your body feels relaxed and loose, slow your vibrating gradually and sit quietly.

❻ Observe your pulse, breath, and mind. Calm your breathing and focus your mind on your lower abdomen.

❼ While sitting and resting, focus intently on your pulse, breath, and mind. Feel gravity pulling your body toward the Earth, and feel the circulation of energy throughout your body. Focus on your abdomen to pull the energy toward your body's center.

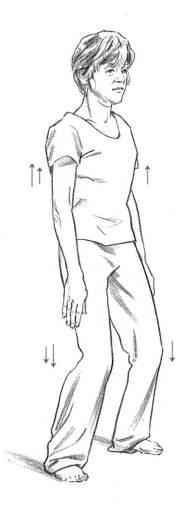

Creativity Exercises

True creativity comes from an integrated brain. It requires a meeting of the rational, emotional, and spiritual that gives rise to something of meaning that satisfies all sides of the human mind. But to do this, you must step outside of the trap of your own preconceptions, to see something new in a new way. Try these exercises to help unleash your creative power.

MUSIC DRAWING

This exercise will help you to feel music deeply and to express yourself spontaneously. You will need three large peices of paper and some crayons.

1. Gather 3 stylistically distinct instrumental songs. For example, try a lighthearted polka, a soft lullaby, or a booming orchestra piece.
2. Sit comfortably with eyes closed, quietly listening to one of the songs. Notice any colors or feelings that come to mind.
3. Gather crayons whose colors best seem to represent the song.
4. Now play the song again, this time "drawing it." Let your hand move freely in response to the music. Do the same for the other 2 songs.

 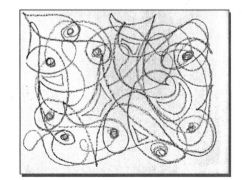

GIBBERISH

This game can be done alone, but it is good for a few extra laughs when done with a friend. Even though you are constantly making noise, you will find that your mind empties during the exercise, which in turn makes room for creative ways of thinking.

1. Look in the mirror into your own eyes or into the eyes of a partner.
2. Begin to carry on a conversation of nonsense words, including all of the requisite gestures and facial expressions. Continue for as long as feels natural, until your "conversation" is over.

ENERGY DANCE

This exercise will increase your energy awareness while also releasing your natural inner grace and expressiveness. You should practice the Feeling Energy exercise on page 68 before attempting this.

1. Sit comfortably on the floor in a half lotus position.
2. Follow the directions for the Feeling Energy exercise on page 68.
3. Focusing on the palms, allow your hands to follow the flow of energy freely. You will feel the whole body move naturally. This is the beginning of energy dance.
4. Let your body move naturally with the flow of energy. It is ideal to have background music that can naturally lead the body movement while practicing.

Energy-Building Exercises

These exercises are meant to build your internal energy system. They could be considered Brain Sensitizing exercises because of their strong effects on the body, but they will also assist you in your process of transformation. They can be used to build strength, stamina, vitality, and will power as you work toward new goals. Some of them can be quite demanding, but stick with them. You'll be surprised by how much better you feel.

UP-THE-WALL ENERGIZER

When we feel fatigued, we don't usually want to move our bodies. However these times are when we need exercise most. When you don't have enough stamina to complete your exercise routine, try this simple but powerful energy- building exercise.

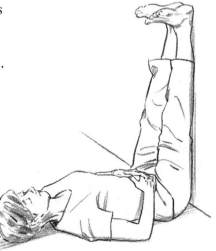

1. Lie on your back with your buttocks close to the wall and your legs elevated and resting against the wall.
2. Place your hands on your abdomen. If this pose causes discomfort because your hamstrings are tight, move your buttocks a few inches away from the wall.

③ Stretch and straighten both legs up to the best of your ability. Flex your feet and push out your heels.

④ Keep your head on the floor and your lower back as close to the floor as possible. Breathe deeply into your abdomen.

⑤ Close your eyes and focus on the energy flow inside your body.

ENERGY ACCUMULATOR

This exercise will help you feel strong, grounded, and centered. Through this exercise, you can grow your personal strength and integrity.

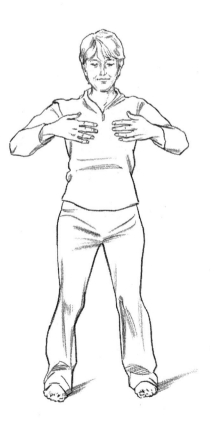

① Stand with your feet shoulder width apart and parallel. Make sure that your weight is distributed evenly so that it rests firmly over the soles of both feet.

② Gently tuck in your tailbone.

③ Relaxing your upper body, raise your hands to chest height, and spread them apart about one foot.

④ Imagine that you have a ball of energy between your hands and your chest.

⑤ Concentrate on your lower abdomen and maintain this posture for about 3 to 5 minutes.

SLEEPING TIGER

This exercise is designed to strengthen, rejuvenate, and energize the body.

1. Lie comfortably on the floor.
2. Lift your arms straight into the air with your palms facing the ceiling. Bend your elbows slightly and flex your wrists back.
3. Lift your legs off the floor, creating 90-degree angles at the hips and knee joints. Keep your feet parallel and your legs parted at shoulder width. Flex your ankles back so that your toes are pulled slightly back toward your head.
4. Breathe comfortably with your lower abdomen. Hold this posture for one minute and gradually add time to it. When you are familiar with this posture, hold it as long as you can.

PUSH-UPS

Push-ups are an old-fashioned exercise, but their benefit remains as real as ever. This exercise will help you gain confidence in your body and mind. Start with a small number and then work up to a larger goal.

1. Place your palms on the floor, directly under your shoulders. Keep your body perfectly straight as you push it off the floor.
2. Bend your elbows at a 90-degree angle as you lower your body to the floor. Keep your back and legs straight and your feet together. At first you can place your knees on the ground if this is difficult.
3. Push back up to the starting position and repeat.
4. Perform as many push-ups as you can.

CHAPTER 5

Your Masterful Brain

Teach us to live our lives with purpose and with power
for visions of a better world and for decision's hour;
To choose the way of life, reject the way of death,
until the radiant force of God fills mind and strength and breath.
—Walter J. Mathams

We conclude with a look at Brain Mastering, the collected disciplines of BEST, which, when practiced as a lifestyle, will give you greater control over your brain and a greater ability to achieve cherished goals. But first, a brief story…

In the ancient Native American tale of Jumping Mouse, a mouse once lived with other mice in their village, and he spent all his time as other mice did: gathering seeds, moving pebbles, and running about. But all the time he heard a strange roaring sound. When he mentioned it to the other mice, they scoffed at him. But eventually, Jumping Mouse had to find out what the roaring sound was. He met Raccoon, who took him to the Great River, where he met Brother Frog. Frog told him that if he wanted medicine of his own, he should jump as high as he could. Jumping Mouse jumped and saw the sacred mountains, and that is how he got his name.

Once he had seen the mountains, Jumping Mouse went back to his people to tell them about his vision. But they would not listen to him. They could not see through his eyes. They could only perceive what others before them had perceived. So Jumping Mouse set off alone to find the sacred mountains. Jumping Mouse gave his eyes to other animals in order that they should see, which left him blind. With their help, he continued his quest. Finally, he reached the summit of the sacred mountain and found the great lake where all the world is reflected. Left alone with only his sense of touch, Jumping Mouse was content, knowing the great Eagle would finally get him. An eagle swooped down, he heard a rush of wings, and everything went black.

Suddenly, Jumping Mouse awoke and realized he could see colors. A voice asked him if he wanted medicine, and he said yes. The voice told him to jump as high as he could. The wind caught him and took him high into the air, where he could see Buffalo and Raccoon and the medicine lake and the sacred mountain. He saw his friend Frog by the lake and called down to him, "Hello, Brother Frog." The frog called back, "Hello, Brother Eagle!"

Completing Your Transformation

This story is universal. By opening their minds and seeking beyond themselves, wanderers come to a wider wisdom, a larger view not only of the world but of themselves. They learn to give and to be enlarged by the act of giving. Others may scoff and misunderstand their intentions, but in the end, they are transformed.

This is the essence of your journey. As someone who has lived five, six, seven decades or more, you have probably found that you were expected to adhere to a set of predetermined ideas. But all the while, you have wondered if there was a way you could escape the limitations of your thought habits and become a larger person with greater vision.

There is. It's Brain Mastering, in which the skills and concepts you have learned throughout the first four stages of BEST come together as a single unified discipline.

A Spiritual Quest

BEST is a spiritual quest—a quest to become a person of greater enlightenment as you make the transition into the mature years of your life. You have plenty of goals: to heal from the traumas of the past, to find peace, to develop a healthier body, and even to discover a new purpose for your life. Brain Mastering is discovering the life you want to live and developing a mental discipline that allows you to turn your brain into a tool to create that life. It is a continual process of improving your brain to become a better human being.

Essayist Sidney Smith said, "Regret for the things we did can be tempered by time; it is regret for the things we did not do that is inconsolable." Many of us struggle with regrets about the things we have not done in our lives. These regrets become more acute and painful as we age, like a disease that eats away at the peace and serenity of many older people, turning what should be a time of exploration, vitality, and joy into a shadowy country of unfulfilled promises and resentment.

With Brain Mastery, you can break free from the unrealized goals of your past. You become a new person with new perspectives and a new ability to harness the creative and reasoning powers of your brain. Free from past fears, prejudices, and preconceptions, you can create a new future and do after seventy the things that you wanted to do at thirty-five. Have you read about those men and women in their seventies and beyond who are climbing the Himalayas, winning literary awards, and starting world-changing charities? There's nothing in them that is not in you. You cannot go back and rewrite chapter one, but you can start now to make a fantastic finale.

Master of the House

Through the continual, lifelong practice of Brain Mastering, you will truly become master of your brain. This means building a lifestyle centered in part on the four previous stages of BEST. You will continue to engage in Brain Sensitizing, Versatilizing, Refreshing, and Integrating. As you do, over time you will continue to create new neural pathways that will help you discover new abilities and new ways of thinking. In short, you will find new solutions to the problems of living.

This new lifestyle can truly lead to a new life! For example, if you were not previously interested in writing, but then in your brain education journey you discover an urge to write your memoirs, you might find yourself in writers' workshops, meeting other writers, and engaging your creativity to the fullest. Who knows, you could be a published writer for the first time in your seventies. The important thing is that you tried something new.

Brain Mastering makes maturity what it should be: a prime time of life when you are free of the constraints of work and children and are free to pursue a rich, rewarding existence. So many older adults miss out on this time because they cling to old grudges or let their minds become frail and halting, but that is a fate to which no one need be consigned. Science is showing us that our minds, emotions, and attitudes affect how long and how well we live as much as, or more than, what we eat or how much we exercise. A positive, hopeful, curious mind is a resource for exploring all the wonders that later life has to offer: Want to travel? Go back to school and get your master's degree? Start a company? Volunteer? Learn to meditate? Do it. When you are master of your brain, you are master of your life.

You might also inspire others. Not all people who reach maturity will hear of BEST on their own. Some short-sighted people might even consider it New Age mumbo-jumbo. We know the truth: You must grow older, but you don't have to grow old. You can just grow—in sagacity, purpose, joy, and energy. By pursuing your Brain Mastering lifestyle, you may well motivate others to do the same. You may change one life or a dozen.

Finding Your Purpose

An article in the publication *AdultSpan Journal* tells us, "A focus on meaning and purpose provides a positive, optimistic perspective that is counter to disempowering views of aging based on losses and deficits." For many years, gerontologists and sociologists have believed that having purpose and meaning in later life is a key to longevity and health. To see how true this is, observe the difference between the ways in which two mature individuals cope with retirement. One leaves her full-time job and dives into volunteer work, painting, church work, and travel. She feels useful and energized and meets new people. The other person leaves his job and plays golf. This grows boring, so he sits and watches television. His mind slows. He becomes isolated and angry. Which person do you think lives longer and better?

Purpose is essential to life. The Purpose Project at the Center for Spirituality and Healing at the University of Minnesota validates this idea: A sense of purpose and meaning give us the will to live. With it, you are practically indomitable; time becomes meaningless as you cherish each moment. Without it, well, you're just taking up space.

Now that you have begun to discover the kind of person you want to become, you are free to begin discovering your life's purpose based on your clearer perceptions of who you are and who you can become. You will use your revitalized brain to find your true potential as an entrepreneur, creator, grandparent, healer—whatever you want to be. So ask yourself, what are your goals? Some questions to get you started:

- What have I always wanted to do?
- What is my passion in life?
- Do I feel fulfilled?
- What do I value most in life?
- What do I see as the meaning of my life?
- What would I like to achieve in the next ten years?
- What would I like my legacy to be?

The meaning of your life is up to you. What an opportunity! So think about what fires your passions. Think about what you could do every day for the next twenty years without ever becoming bored. Then make it happen. Your brain, now fully awakened, has the ability to change your world and the world around you.

Meditation for Life

Meditation is a very powerful tool for Brain Mastering. Meditation has been practiced for thousands of years in cultures throughout the world. Some meditate by altering their thoughts; others use breathing or muscle relaxation. Some cultures use psychoactive substances to aid their meditation; others rely on hunger or sleep deprivation. But the goal of all meditation is the same: to quiet the conscious mind.

As intellectual beings, we create and receive a nonstop stream of information from our brains and the world around us. This "noise" overwhelms our brains and minds so that we cannot hear the voices within us. Meditation stills the flow of conscious thought—analysis, questioning, and self-talk—and simply lets the mind be. This activates other parts of our brains and allows us to begin perceiving things in a different way.

Meditation requires training, especially for Western minds, which are so immersed in the empirical. In the West, we are taught to distrust what our intuition tells us. But more ancient societies know that often meditation and self-awareness are powerful ways to learn about life, the cosmos, and the Self. A blend of Western scientific knowledge and ancient wisdom is the ideal way to gain understanding. Meditation is a wonderful place to begin, but it is also a practice that takes time and patience. It is worth your time to find a teacher or mentor who can help you build a meditative skill set.

There are two basic types of meditation. In concentrative meditation, the meditator focuses the mind on the breath and uses a mantra or sound in order to shut out all other stimuli. In mindful meditation, the meditator opens the mind to all sensation but thinks about none of them; he or she merely experiences. There are hundreds of subcategories of meditation; let your mind and spirit guide you to the method that is right for you.

The Power of Mental Intention

Meditation has the amazing ability to transform the brain. In 2004, a group of brain scientists, neurologists, and Buddhist monks met at the Dalai Lama's home in India to answer a burning question: Can pure thought and intent affect the structure of the brain? By this time it had been accepted that repeated physical actions could alter the brain. But could mental intention? Remember, most Western neuroscientists believe that the mind is just the activity of the brain, nothing more. In this view, intention does not exist. So scientists and master meditators came together to learn whether the brain could change in response to purely internal, mental signals.

A group of monks who had spent a total of more than ten thousand hours in meditation entered a meditative state of compassion, in which they generated a feeling of loving kindness toward all living things. Magnetic resonance imaging (MRI) scans showed striking results: The experienced meditators showed a dramatic jump in the brainwaves that indicate high brain activity, increases larger than anything ever seen in neuroscience at the time.

Just as intriguing was the fact that the activity in the left prefrontal cortex, which is associated with positive emotions, overwhelmed the right prefrontal cortex, where negative emotions reside. The researchers had never seen this caused by purely mental activity. The evidence was clear: Focused thought can alter the brain.

Some people will claim that meditation is pagan, anti-Christian, or other things. These opinions are misinformed. Meditation is actually non-denominational; it supports all religious traditions by encouraging self-truth and contemplation. What's more, meditation has been proven to improve longevity, help with stress management, strengthen the immune system, assist in pain control, lift chronic fatigue, and positively affect a host of other problems. Meditation is a powerful tool that you can use in your quest to become a more enlightened person.

You Decide

As we near the end of our journey together, you will be making decisions about your future—what purpose to pursue, how to live, how to be. You will, of course, try to make good decisions, but here is more good news: As a result of Brain Mastering, you will find yourself becoming more decisive. Because you see clearly—perhaps for the first time—who you truly are and what your potential is, you know what your path should be. You will not hesitate out of fear. You will make sound decisions with confidence and act without apprehension.

Because of this new confidence in your own decision-making ability, you will also find that you are able to form more peaceful relationships. When you are happier with yourself, you will feel no need to engage in arguments or to contest others' views of life. Comfortable in your new self-knowledge, you will feel at peace to engage others on a level of tolerance, understanding, and giving. You will discover that you want not to be right, but to inspire. People who go through BEST often become very interested in helping people.

As you continue with a daily practice of Brain Education System Training, you will continue to develop your mind. Your spirit will mature and evolve. You will live your best life. It doesn't matter whether you are forty, sixty, or past eighty. Your brain is always changing and holds within its cells limitless possibilities for growth and joy.

Follow Your Dream

As you get older, it is as important that you have a dream for your life as it was when you were young. You may have a better chance of achieving it, now that the basics needs of life—financial security, starting a career, raising a family, etc.—are no longer of primary importance to you. So, before you close this book up and put it back on the shelf, make sure that you have developed a vision for yourself. Make a plan for who you want to be one, five, or ten years from now. This does not have to mean starting a new career or taking on some huge project (but that is okay, too). More importantly, it means becoming the kind of person you really want to be in terms of character and your interaction with the world around you. If you have ever thought to yourself, "I want to leave the world a better place than I found it," now is the time to act on that desire.

To find your vision, find what really fills you with a sense of joy and contentment. For most, this will probably involve contributing something of value to your community or the world. Don't be afraid to set your goal high and to dream big.

THE BRAIN-MASTERING LIFESTYLE

Brain Mastering means making the other steps of BEST a daily discipline. But adopting anything as a daily practice can be a challenge. How do you fit these exercises into an already busy life? By designing your lifestyle around your brain. Here are some suggestions for doing this:

• CREATE A SPACE IN YOUR HOME THAT IS EXCLUSIVELY FOR YOUR BEST WORK

Make it a peaceful, meditative space where you can have privacy. Furnish it with whatever you need to feel focused and serene: candles, incense, music, fabrics, pillows, whatever feels right.

• SET ASIDE A SPECIFIC PERIOD OF TIME AS YOUR BEST TIME

If you have been spending an hour per day watching reality TV, turn off the television and instead work on your BEST exercises. Make this something you do every day at the same time. Routine becomes habit in as little as three weeks.

• POST REMINDERS THROUGHOUT YOUR LIVING AND WORKING SPACE

These can be notes to yourself, photographs, or anything that reminds you of the work you need to do.

• WRITE DOWN YOUR GOALS

When you have specific goals in mind, you are much more likely to take supporting actions to reach those goals.

• USE DAILY AFFIRMATIONS

Speaking positive affirmations aloud each morning will clarify your purpose. Saying things such as, "I am a purposeful being, and today I will move one step closer to my full potential," can remind you of what you need to do and fill you with positive motivation.

Meditation Postures

Several studies have shown that very specific, concrete things happen in the brain when you meditate. First of all, your brain waves drop dramatically during meditation to a level very similar to the brain waves emitted during dreaming. You could look at meditation as a kind of waking sleep, a time when you have consciously and purposely allowed your brain to rest and relax deeply. The benefits of this are truly profound, since so many physical ailments are related to stress. You could also look at meditation as happiness training. Dr. Richard Davidson of the University of Wisconsin theorizes that meditation increases activity in the left prefrontal cortex, which is associated with feelings of contentment and joy. The more you practice meditation, the more your brain will gain the habit of using these regions of the brain. Also, scientists have noted that meditation calms activity in the amygdala, which is responsible for fear and stress responses. Before you begin deep meditation, practice these basic postures.

FLOOR MEDITATION POSTURE

This is the classic half-lotus meditation posture. If you find it uncomfortable, you can sit on a pillow or against a wall (or both). You can also do this with your legs extended or in a chair.

1. Sit on the floor with your legs crossed. One foot may rest on the floor, but the other should sit on your thigh.

2. Keep your back straight. Place your hands on your knees. Hold your palms facing upward.

3. You may close your eyes or keep them open. Relax your shoulders. Keep your chin slightly lowered.

4. Open your mouth slightly and keep focusing on exhalation. Focus on the energy flow inside your body.

CHAIR MEDITATION POSTURE

1. Sit on a chair comfortably. Keep your legs apart at shoulder width.

2. Place your hands on your abdomen or rest them on your thighs.

3. Relax your chest, shoulders, and arms completely.

4. You may close your eyes or keep them open.

5. Open your mouth slightly and keep focusing on exhalation. Focus on the energy flow inside your body.

Vision Meditation

This meditation helps you supply the brain with information that is positive, refreshing, and supportive–information that will motivate the brain to its full capacity. The most important role of our brain is to help us find ways to fulfill our visions and dreams. Pursuit of a vision will awaken your brain's innate potential and will provide unending motivation worthy of your time and effort.

VISION MEDITATION EXERCISE 1

1. Sit in the half-lotus position and straighten your back. Do Feeling Energy exercise (page 68) for a few minutes.

2. When you feel the surrounding energy field and have quieted your thoughts and emotions, lower your hands to your knees or rest your cupped hands on your heels.

3. Create a picture in your mind of the person you want to be or the goal you want to achieve.

4. Imagine in detail that your desire has already been achieved and give yourself acknowledgment and an assuring message.

5. Concentrate on your lower abdomen; breathe in and out deeply 3 times.

6. Clap quickly 10 times, rub your hands together briskly, and gently massage your face.

VISION MEDITATION EXERCISE 2

❶ Sit in the half-lotus position and straighten your back. Do the Feeling Energy exercise, page 68, for a couple of minutes, until you feel the energy clearly.

❷ When you feel the surrounding energy field, cup your hands above your head, without touching it, and feel the flow of energy emanating from your brain.

❸ As you feel the energy from your brain, spread your fingers apart and bring them in again to expand the feeling of the energy. Bring your hands closer and push them farther out from your head as you feel the force of the energy, like magnetic attraction and repulsion.

❹ Let the movement of your hands, breath, and brain synchronize into one rhythm. Let your body inflate and deflate like a large balloon with the rhythm of your breath.

❺ Create a picture in your mind of the person you want to be or the goal you want to achieve.

❻ Imagine in detail that your desire has already been achieved and give yourself acknowledgment and assurance of success.

❼ Concentrate on your lower abdomen as you breathe in and out deeply 3 times.

❽ Clap quickly 10 times, rub your hands together briskly, and gently massage your face.

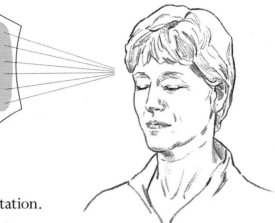

BRAIN SCREEN

1. Set aside a specific time for meditation. Sit comfortably and breathe in and out deeply 3 times.

2. Lift your hands to chest level and begin Feeling Energy exercise (page 68).

3. Once you feel the surrounding energy field and quiet your thoughts and emotions, lower your hands to your knees.

4. Imagine that a stream of energy is entering the top of your head and shooting out from between your eyebrows. Imagine that it is projecting out like a film on a screen in front of you.

5. Visualize yourself being healthy, happy, and peaceful. Genuinely feel these qualities with your entire being.

6. Breathe in and out 3 times and then open your eyes.

Developing Your True Identity

The following exercises will help you examine your current identity, as well as get a better idea of who you would really like to be.

FROM ANOTHER PERSPECTIVE

It can be hard to stand back and really see ourselves as we are. We tend to filter our conception of self through many layers of judgment and wishful thinking. Use this exercise to see yourself from an objective point of view. Describe yourself from the perspective of some non-human thing, such as your couch or your dog. How do you appear from this perspective? Be as honest and complete as possible, referencing your character, appearance, and behavior. Try this from several different perspectives.

IN REMEMBRANCE OF ME

As we get older, it is natural to think occasionally about our own mortality. Rather than letting this be a source of sadness, let it be a source of motivation. If you are in the last decades of your life, it means that there is no more time to waste. You must grow into the person you want to be now. With this attitude, the passage of time can become a great blessing to you.

To help yourself with this, think ahead to how you want to be remembered. Write a eulogy for yourself as you would want it to be delivered at your funeral. This may seem a bit morbid, but it is a helpful exercise for anyone of any age. Take some time to think about what traits you want people to associate with you. Generosity? Courage? Love? Use this exercise to help set your mind toward embodying these traits in your life.

DECLARE YOUR CHARACTER

Through the years, you may have developed some character traits that you would like to change. Or perhaps you have a difficult time remaining positive about yourself or the world around you. Fortunately, all of these things are simply habits of the brain that can be changed with will and persistence.

To begin changing your mindset, create a simple declarative sentence that will keep your mind focused on developing a positive trait. In other words, create a statement that helps you be the kind of person you want to be. This statement should be a declaration of character, a simple "I am" statement. For example, you could say, "I am generous," or, "I am beautiful." Choose whatever trait that you most desire within yourself. Write the declaration on several Post-it notes and put them within easy view—on your computer monitor, your refrigerator, your dashboard—anywhere that you will see it often.

MAKE YOUR MOTTO AND MISSION

Corporations and other large organizations spend a lot of time and money developing the proper identity for their business. These things do a lot to establish how they relate to the world around them. Think about how much more effectively the army can recruit with a slogan like "Be all you can be." And a pair of athletic shoes are so much more attractive with the familiar swoosh and the phrase "Just do it" emblazoned on the box.

Why don't you do the same for yourself? Come up with a short statement, a motto, that sums up your intentions for your life. Also, prepare a mission statement, a paragraph describing your personal vision for the remainder of your life. Perhaps you have pursued and achieved many missions in your life up to this point. Now it is your chance to make one as you really want, one that really will bring you satisfaction and fulfillment.

21-DAY MIRACLE

Good habits are what make your dreams come true. That may seem like an exaggeration, but it is really true. Anything you do will require discipline and effort. If you set your goals high, it can seem overwhelming. That is why you should start with smaller, achievable goals. Eventually they will add up, like bricks building a house.

Identify one habit in your life that you think causes some sort of difficulty for you. Ideally, this should be a purely behavioral issue, rather than one with a chemical component, such as smoking or drinking. Give yourself the challenge of stopping the behavior for 21 days. At the end of 21 days, your dependence on that behavior will have faded along with the neural connections that support it.

Visit www.ilchi.com and you will find special support for your 21-day process, including special 21-day tracking features and details about setting a goal. This online program, 21-Day Miracle, was created to help you build the habits you need to make the life of your dreams. You just need to choose one goal and three rules to follow for 21 days.

AFTERWORD

Embodying the Jangsaeng Ideal

A journey of a thousand miles begins with a single step.
—Lao Tzu

And so we reach the conclusion of our journey in this book, but the beginning of your own journey. It is a long but rewarding journey, and whether you decide to share it with us as part of our BEST coursework or proceed on your own path, your life will be richer as a result.

The journey is not without its obstacles. One of the most daunting is your ingrained way of thinking. By the time we have reached maturity, we tend to be set in our ways. Strong opinions color our emotions. If your mindset is skeptical, regretful, or doubtful of your ability to change your brain, you will not succeed. Therefore, as a parting gift to you, we wish to share the most important state of mind to cultivate as you begin BEST—something we call the Jangsaeng ideal.

There are certain key characteristics of a person who has Jangsaeng, longevity not only of lifespan, but of mind and spirit as well. Through your life, I am sure you have met older, sometimes very old people, who still have an amazing amount of vitality. These are the people who never stop inspiring, never stop connecting, and never stop loving their time on this Earth. These are the Jangsaeng people...and you can be one of them.

If you really want to be a Jangsaeng person, it is not a matter of luck or genetics. Rather, Jangsaeng is a light that continually pours forth from the inner world of these people that we so greatly admire and love. The BEST method is found on the notion that health, happiness, and peace are not traits we inherit, but choose. These things are not out there somewhere waiting to be found by random chance, nor can they be granted to us by someone else. Rather they are all right here, right now, waiting for our brains to open up to them. The ravages of time can do a lot to reduce the mechanisms of the body, but it can never do anything to lessen this kind of spirit. To have this sort of power, focus on these basic human ideals:

GRATITUDE—Remind yourself each day to wallow in gratitude for all that you have and to be humble because you have received such gifts. You are alive, and with life come potential and hope. You have your health, even if it is not perfect. You have a body that, despite its flaws, is still capable of creating so much and experiencing so much in this world. You have people in your life who love and cherish you. And you have a marvelous brain that can reshape your life according to your vision. Feel gratitude for all these things daily and share your graditude with others. It is the best antidote to cynicism that we know.

LOVING-KINDNESS—This principle means possessing a sense of deep caring and acceptance of all others, no matter how different from you they appear to be. Because in reality, we are all one. You may have felt this directly in your meditation. In any case, such powerful unconditional love of all your brothers and sisters will elevate your being.

COURAGE—Never make decisions out of fear. Remember, the word *fear* means "False Evidence Appearing Real." When you act out of fear, it is almost always because something is telling you that you are less capable than you are. Remember this and act with courage when you are confronted by a decision. Take an intelligent risk. Do something new. Break your pattern. Speak out.

OPENNESS—One of the strongest human impulses is the desire to feel that we know, that we have the answers. This is the drive that leads people to fundamentalism and intolerance. When your way becomes the only way, you will distrust those who do not share your beliefs. Instead, remember that it is the mysteries of life that give it meaning. Exploring and learning, not static knowledge, make living exciting. Embrace the mysteries of faith, science, and spirituality and enjoy the fact that there is so much that you do not know.

GENEROSITY—Making a difference in the life of another is one of the greatest purposes a human being can have. Each day, try to figure out not what you can take, but what you can give. Seek ways to give some of what you have and thank the world for all it has given you. This may mean volunteering for a local nonprofit organization, helping someone who is disabled, or regularly donating to charities. But make generosity part of your routine. Teach it to younger members of your family as often as you can.

FORGIVENESS—Forgiving others for past offenses is healing for you and for them. Reconsider old grudges and rivalries and ask yourself if there is any value in holding on to them. It is unlikely. Instead, forgiveness enriches your life and the lives of those you pardon. Leave the past in the past and turn the page. It truly is a divine act.

INTEGRITY—In the later third of life, you are in a perfect position to reflect upon where you have been and where you are headed. Thus, you can examine to what degree your words and actions of the past and present agree with the inner framework of your value system. Undoubtedly, you will find some lack of consistency between the two. Now is your chance to live fully integrated with your highest ideals, and more importantly to be completely true to your highest sense of self.

HEALTH—Finally, focus your mind on the health of all things: the Earth, yourself, and those around you. This means eating well and exercising, but it goes beyond that. It means living in ways that preserve the planet, which usually means living simply. We have much more than we need; most of us could live with far less money and far more joy by peeling away some of the layers of material possession from our lives. By orienting your thoughts toward what is healthy, simple, and beautiful, you will find your body and mind blooming.

Brain Education System Training is more than a program or a course of study. It is a way of living. Engage in it to the fullest and you will find yourself more aware and more alive than you ever thought possible. The power of successful aging lies within you. It is about how active and healthy you are, how well you adapt to change, how connected with others you remain, how much you devote yourself to the welfare of others, and how you define your purpose in life. Generosity, kindness, compassion, and patience are not only ethical choices; they are essential to successful aging. Live with love, live long, and live happy.

Walk Yourself Young: Jangsaeng Walking

1. Introduction

You might say that Jangsaeng Walking began as a "lucky break." I (Ilchi Lee) was horseback riding one day when the horse came to an abrupt stop, and I was catapulted off, sustaining serious injuries for which doctors prescribed a full month of bed rest.

Having always been extraordinarily active and healthy, as well as having helped people heal their bodies for nearly thirty years, I was determined to get started healing my own. While I respected the doctor's opinion and recommendation of bed rest, I began hatching a plan to get my body moving again the moment the doctor left the room. Though any movement was excruciatingly painful, I began by simply breathing deeply and making small movements. Within one day of the accident, I was able to take a few standing steps.

Over the next few months, as I worked to bring life back into my injured body, the Jangsaeng Walking method came to life as well.

Forced to slow down because of my injury, I was able to observe my body in different ways than I had before. As I walked, I noticed that my posture and body angles had changed over the years, from that of a confident, young man, walking upright, to that of an "old man," upper body leaning backwards, head back, and body weight on my heels.

When I complained of these changes in my body to others, they simply replied, "Of course. You're getting old."

But this sort of defeatist attitude did not settle well with me. After all, it is in complete contradiction to everything I have taught my students over the past twenty-six years. "My body is not me, but mine," I tell them to tell themselves. Somehow, though, I had let my body start to call the shots. I had never told my body, "Okay, you are old now. It's time to start walking like an old man." Yet, somehow it happened anyway. Basically, it happened because I let it happen. It was time to put myself in the driver's seat once again.

With this realization, I resolved not only to heal my body from the accident, but to reform the habits I had developed. I began paying close attention to the angles and posture of my body as I walked. I decided that I was one to decide how and when to grow old, and it didn't have to happen in the ways people normally assume.

I closely observed how my body felt in different positions as I carefully made one step at a time. I was like a baby learning to walk. I also observed how people around me walked. I noticed that the young and the old usually have distinct ways of walking. When I asked students to make slight changes in the way they walked, their bodies' alignment improved dramatically. By tilting forward slightly and pressing on the ball of the foot, practitioners were able to correct problems in the knee, hip joint, and pelvis.

So, I decided the best way to start feeling young again was to start walking youthfully. I was forced to resume a full lecture tour schedule shortly after the accident. The pain in my spine was still quite intense, but I made a concerted effort to apply the walking and posture principles I had developed. Applying what I had learned through the years, I deliberately shifted my posture to accommodate better energy flow. After about five months, this way of walking became a habit in my life.

Eventually, I started feeling like my body was full of vibrant energy, as if I were young again. My body felt unbelievably light, my movement became quick, and I became nearly unaware of my injured back. I discovered the joy of walking and looked for chances to take increasingly long and more frequent walks. This way of walking not only helped me return to my previous level of health, but I now feel ten years younger than I did at the time of my accident. I named the walking style Jangsaeng Walking, which roughly translates to longevity walking, because I feel it has restored youth and vitality to my body.

WALK YOUR WAY TO WELLNESS

Walking is a perfect path to wellness. Basically, it can be done anywhere at any time and, more importantly, it works. Numerous studies have confirmed that walking—any kind of walking—is tremendously good for the body.

Walking is a whole body exercise that uses more than six hundred muscles and two hundred bones that move along with those muscles. Walking stimulates countless nerves that are spread throughout the body through the soles. It strengthens the lower body muscles by vigorously promoting blood circulation in the legs and intestines.

First of all, please accept that walking is real exercise. One unfortunate misconception is that exercise needs to be extremely intense to work at all. People commonly think they are not really working out unless they are sweating profusely and every muscle of their body is aching. This is simply not the case and, in fact, bursts of intense exercise may actually be detrimental for all but the most highly trained athletes.

Most health experts agree that people should work out at about sixty-five to eighty-five percent of their maximum heart rate. This seems to be the training zone in which individuals experience the greatest health benefits, in particular increasing cardiovascular fitness and body fat reduction. If you interrupt your sedentary lifestyle with sudden bouts of high-impact aerobics or sprinting, you might not be helping yourself, and you may be doing more harm than good. Walking at a steady, moderate pace will help you achieve and maintain the ideal heart rate quickly and easily.

A PRACTICAL SOLUTION

And the greatest aspect of walking is its practicality. Walking requires no special equipment or clothing, and it can be done at just about any place and any time. Even the busiest person can find time to work it into a schedule. Just start by finding creative ways to add more steps to your day, and soon you will find that you have doubled your level of physical activity without ever paying a single gym membership or buying any sort of fitness gadget.

If you are used to thinking that your exercise routine must happen in long, sustained bouts several times a week, think again. A recent study suggests that short "exercise snacks" are a way to boost your cardiovascular fitness and to keep excess fat off your body. In other words, the thirty to sixty minutes of exercise you need do not have to happen all at once; they can happen in short ten- to fifteen-minute increments throughout the day.

You can easily apply this concept to walking since it is something you already do every day anyway. Simply find ways to add steps to your day, to create "walking snacks" throughout your day. For example, instead of circling around the parking lot looking for the closest parking space, park at the outer edge of the lot, and apply Jangsaeng Walking as you walk toward the building. Or get in the habit of standing up and walking around in proper posture whenever you receive a cell phone call.

THE JANGSAENG STYLE

The word *jangsaeng*, in fact, means "youthful longevity," which reflects the goal of this walking style. Walking in general has been shown to add healthy years to people's lives, but I think this benefit can be accentuated by paying careful attention to the way you walk. My hypothesis is essentially that you can return your body and your energy system to a more youthful state simply by walking in a more youthful way.

Jangsaeng Walking helps to reestablish the proper Water Up, Fire Down condition by moving the body and by stimulating the Yong-chun point on the bottom of the foot. Energy goes down to the sole naturally as we walk while focusing on Yong-chun, which helps to relieve the undesirable Fire Up condition. Fire energy, which is accumulated under stressful conditions, is brought down to the feet, causing the soles to get warmer. As you walk, you may even notice a burning sensation on the soles of your feet as this process occurs. This action essentially redirects fire energy away from the head, and the brain is able to become cool and clear once again.

If you walk in the Jangsaeng style regularly, your energy will begin to calm down automatically, and your mind will stay clear and focused. The body and the brain can function better when you maintain this condition.

GETTING A LEG UP ON THE COMPETITION

In Korea, we have a saying: "Healthy legs, long life." The legs may in fact be the source of strength and vitality in the body. The vitality of the body depends on the amount of muscle mass, and approximately thirty percent of the body's muscle mass is concentrated in the legs. Athletes have over forty percent muscle mass in the legs. The more muscle mass you have, the more energy you have. By contrast, the less muscle mass you have, the less energy you will have.

When the legs get weak, you feel that moving the body itself is difficult and cumbersome. This creates a vicious cycle of inactivity leading to more inactivity. If you sit around because you feel weak, your muscle mass lessens and you become more weak. The aging process of the legs rapidly progresses due to prolonged lack of exercise, and eventually it becomes difficult to even sit down and stand up, which is the picture of old age that we all dread.

To be alive is to move. Be appreciative about the fact that you have two legs that can sustain the body, that you can go anywhere on them, and move your legs in earnest. The more you move them, the stronger the muscles will get.

2. The Jangsaeng Method

In Eastern thought, there is a saying, "Where the mind goes, energy follows." Essentially, energy flows following our conscious thought. In fact, everything that we accomplish in this world begins with a conscious thought. For example, if you admire a tall building in the middle of the city, you can say that it all began in the mind of the architect working in tandem with the investors, contractors, and workers who brought it into being. As all these minds came together, energy began to flow toward the fulfillment of the vision. In that way, imagination became reality. Every space mission, every classic piece of art, every saintly act began as a thought in someone's mind.

MIND OVER MATTER

The same is true for the energy we feel in our bodies. When imagining that we can feel energy through our hands, it really happens that way, and if we imagine that energy is collected in the lower abdomen, then energy is really collected in the lower abdomen. One can only feel energy by focusing the consciousness—not by knowledge, analysis, or judgment.

Jangsaeng Walking is partially based on this notion that energy follows the mind. Part of the goal is to teach the body to walk youthfully, which might be something you have never really done since bad habit can start early. Through walking youthfully, your body will regain the attributes of youth, as will your mind. Finally, my hope is that this feeling of energetic youthfulness will follow you into all areas of your life, creating a more vital and satisfying style of life.

ANGLES

Although the mind is important to the creation of a young energy age, one cannot ignore the body itself. Energy travels through the body in a definite way, and it only makes sense to work with it, not against it. For that reason, the Jangsaeng method advocates specific angles of the body to consider when walking. You may be used to walking unconsciously, so at first this may seem a little burdensome. But after a little practice, it will become automatic and will feel completely natural.

OVERVIEW OF JANGSAENG WALKING POSTURE

The basic posture of Jangsaeng Walking is simple. Walk while focusing on these basic principles:

- Tilt the lower part of your pelvis forward.
- Breathe with your lower abdomen.
- Let your heel tap the ground gently as you step forward, with a straight leg.
- Feel your weight transfer fully to the balls (Yong-chun) and toes of your foot.
- Keep your feet parallel, stepping on either side of an imaginary line.
- Angle your body one degree forward.
- Swing your arms freely.
- Smile!

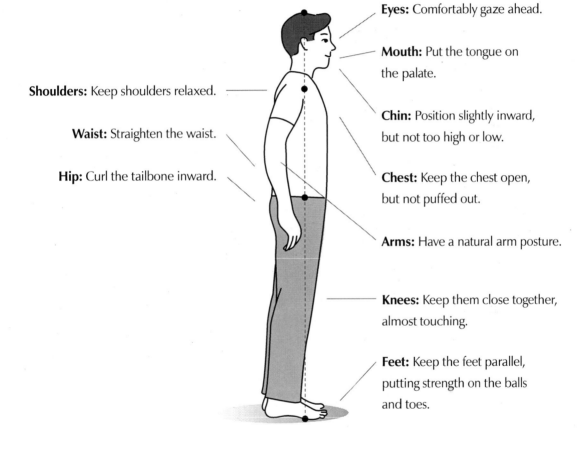

Eyes: Comfortably gaze ahead.

Mouth: Put the tongue on the palate.

Chin: Position slightly inward, but not too high or low.

Chest: Keep the chest open, but not puffed out.

Arms: Have a natural arm posture.

Knees: Keep them close together, almost touching.

Feet: Keep the feet parallel, putting strength on the balls and toes.

Shoulders: Keep shoulders relaxed.

Waist: Straighten the waist.

Hip: Curl the tailbone inward.

The Basic Posture of Jangsaeng Walking

JANGSAENG WALKING PRINCIPLE 1: *Step Symmetrically*

Spend a few minutes observing how you walk normally. Notice if one leg takes more weight, or of there is pain on one side. Also notice your footsteps. You may notice that one or both feet turn inward or outward. The feet should remain consistently parallel, like the number eleven. If not, it is an indication that the legs are not in proper alignment with the pelvis.

This sort of misalignment can lead to serious problems in the knee and hip joints. Also, when the legs are not aligned, they consume more energy in each step. While walking, consciously try to keep your legs parallel with your knees turned forward. Your knees should almost touch, and the legs and feet should remain parallel throughout the entire step.

In the human body, the pelvis is to the body like the foundation is to a building. When properly aligned, the rest of the body will naturally follow. Carefully aligning your legs and feet in this way will help facilitate energy flow in the legs, and it will allow better accumulation of energy in the abdomen, which is the center of physical energy. Digestion and circulation around the organs will also improve as the entire body comes back into alignment, thereby improving your overall sense of well-being.

Walking with the body symmetrical is the most basic principle of Jangsaeng Walking, and it governs the whole circulation system of the body and energy. When feeling tired or powerless at work, or when you feel pain and stiffness in the joints, focus on realigning your body for better energy flow. You will feel much better.

CHECKPOINT

- ☑ Make sure your feet stay parallel.
- ☑ Step forward dynamically while letting the knees touch each other and the toes point forward.

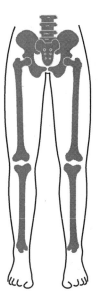
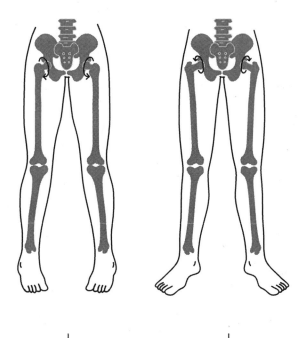

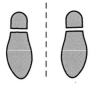
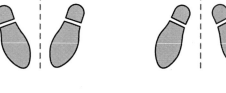

Jangsaeng position   Incorrect foot position leads to loss of energy.

JANGSAENG WALKING PRINCIPLE 2: *Activate the Wellspring*

In Oriental medicine, the Yong-chun is one of the most important energy points. Yong-chun means "like spring water spouts out of the earth, life energy is created inside the body." It is believed to be a source of great vitality and courage for your life. This same concept is represented in the West in the term "cold feet," which suggests that courage is somehow connected to circulation in the feet.

Yong-chun is located in the front third of the sole, right under the ball of the foot, between the second and big toes. It is located in the indention where the sole print creates an upside-down V shape.

To stimulate the Yong-chun, stand up straight and comfortably, and lean forward about one degree from the center of the sole. When standing this way, your weight naturally shifts to the Yong-chun. As you do this, concentrate on your Yong-chun and use the strength of your toes. Since the weight is now evenly distributed throughout the body, the joints won't have the burden of bearing your entire weight. You may notice that it is hard to stand still in this posture because your body will want to spring forward naturally with little effort.

Now walk forward, concentrating on the Yong-chun and using the strength of your toes, as if you were grabbing the earth. As your weight is placed on your toes, all the weight that was on the heels will move to the front.

When you consciously press on the Yong-chun, you must work the soleus muscle, which is the muscle on the back of the leg near the heel. It is thought that weakness in this muscle may be partly responsible for physical instability in older people. A weak soleus muscle may be responsible for the shuffling gate you often see among the elderly, and it could lead to danger-ous falls. When you press forward on your toes during Jangsaeng Walking, however, you automatically work the soleus muscle.

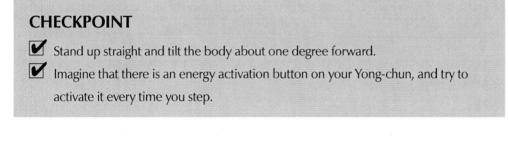

Yong-chun

Jangsaeng Walking

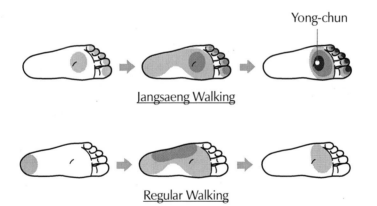

Regular Walking

Patterns of Weight Shifting During Walking

JANGSAENG WALKING PRINCIPLE 3: *Position for Power*

One of the reasons to curl the tailbone is to make the best angle for the energy to be collected in the Dahnjon (lower abdomen), which is the energy center of the body. When the tailbone is curled, and the anus tightens, the hip is naturally lifted upward. Then energy is naturally collected in the Dahnjon, and the rotated pelvis becomes aligned. When the rotated pelvis becomes aligned, the spine is straightened, and the functions of all the organs, including the digestive and genital organs, are improved. Most people's tendency to let the tailbone relax backward, which leads to a great loss of accumulated energy.

Curling up the tailbone is simple. All you need to do is tilt your lower part of your pelvis forward. pull your hips forward a little bit. If you want to check yourself, step up next to a wall, and place your hand between your lower back and the wall. Feel your hand get sandwiched, as you tilt your lower pelvis. Once you've mastered this first step, the rest of the technique will follow more easily.

When curling up the tailbone, the anus tightens, and at this time, the water energy of the kidneys in the back goes upward through the spine and spouts out on the top of the head, as if it's a stream of water that suddenly receives water pressure and rises powerfully. As this water stream envelopes the entire body and flows down, the head that once felt heavy and hot starts feeling cooled down, and eyes that were once bloodshot become clear. The face and skin become lustrous, the mouth that was once dry moistens with saliva, and the mind calms. All these happenings are caused by the energy that pours out at the time of curling the tailbone.

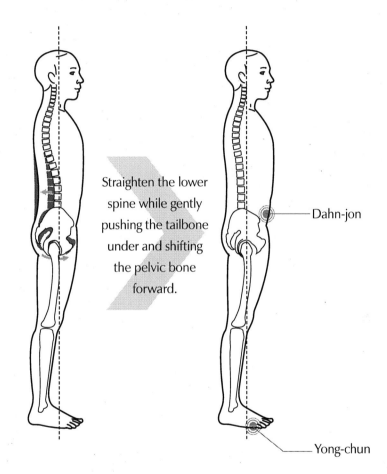

Straighten the lower spine while gently pushing the tailbone under and shifting the pelvic bone forward.

Dahn-jon

Yong-chun

Body Alignment for Jangsaeng Walking

JANGSAENG WALKING PRINCIPLE 4: *Walk with Joy*

If you bend your head backward or forward, the weight of the head pushes down on the cervical vertebra, and it negatively impacts breathing. The cervical vertebra straightens when pulling the chin slightly outward and gazing ahead, then the energy flow into the brain becomes smoother.

Lifting or lowering the head significantly impacts the body. The neck is a crucial pathway where the energy and blood of the body flow into the brain through the meridians, blood vessels, and nerves. Putting the head backward so much that the chin is lifted or putting the head down deeply blocks the passage from the body to the brain, and the energy and blood stop circulating well. The weighty burden on the cervical vertebra causes bad circulation, muscle aches, and eventually imbalance of the entire spine.

When we look at people walking joyfully with their chin up, we too feel good. When you walk joyfully, your mind and body will become young as well. Straighten your back and walk with confidence and joy. But either putting too much stress on the sole, making a loud footstep sound, or walking so lightly that you can barely tell if your sole is touching the ground scatters the energy of the Dahnjon. Therefore, pay special attention to keeping your footsteps moderate in speed and force.

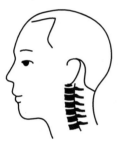

(O)

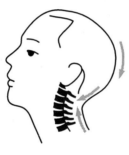

(X)

(X)

Jangsaeng head posture

Tilting the head too far backward or
too far forward blocks energy flow.

JANGSAENG WALKING PRINCIPLE 5: *Engage Your Body*

It is easy to think that we walk only with our feet and we hold things only with our hands, but it is a mistake. Even the easiest and simplest movement is made with every single bone and muscle corresponding to each other and only then do we feel healthy and comfortable. Therefore in every single step we take, we should make sure that all our body parts—including the hip joint, back, shoulders, and arms—correspond to each other.

People who walk with their hands in their pockets and heads down have stiff shoulders, and their necks are putting all the burden of walking on their backs. Eventually the hip joint becomes stiff. The right posture must be the foundation in order to walk for the benefit of the entire body. Keep in mind the basic posture of Jangsaeng Walking, and walk with the feeling of linking the Yong-chun on the sole to the top of the head. Walking with the conscious mind on our body itself is a great health method.

As we continue to walk linking the energy from Yong-chun to our brain, we soon come to feel the rhythm of our own body. Walk joyfully and naturally ride on that rhythm. Focus on your mind and body while walking. We can finally feel inner peace and can make better judgments more objectively outside of our own emotions. When the rhythm is alive in our inner world, our own sensation awakens, and creative ideas are actively generated.

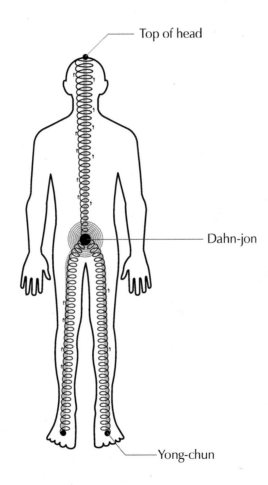

Proper positioning can facilitate circulation of
energy throughout the body.

3. The Walking Brain

All exercise is good for the brain. After all, a healthy body is the starting place for a healthy brain. If our body is healthy, then our circulation of blood to the brain is also good, and it is through the blood that the brain receives all its nutrients and oxygen. The same things that affect the body's health, like cardiovascular fitness and blood sugar levels, all have an effect on the brain. If you develop habits that help you avoid ailments and diseases like heart disease, cancer, and stroke, you will also be doing the body a lot of good.

THE FLEXIBLE BRAIN

But the story of the brain does not end there. Unlike other organs, the brain is unique in its ability to change itself through time. At one time, we used to think that the brain was genetically hardwired by the time we reach adulthood, but that is not the case. Rather, the brain has an ability called neuroplasticity that allows it to continuously revise its connection to adapt to new situations. Ultimately, while your brain does succumb to some effects of aging, it never loses the ability to learn and improve itself.

For that reason, we should not only look at the brain's metabolic functioning when exercising, but we should also consider that which will develop and maintain our neural connections through life. You have the power to design a fitness regimen for yourself that will maximize and maintain flexibility and quickness of the brain.

Physical movement of any type is a good place to start. Any time we move our body, a host of neural connections is activated, and various parts of the brain are stimulated. A sedentary person is doing his brain little good since relatively few neurons are activated when we remain sitting. A sedentary lifestyle essentially allows the brain connections to atrophy, becoming sluggish or even inaccessible, especially as one gets older. An active person, on the other hand, is continually reinforcing the complex interaction of brain impulses needed to facilitate movement.

Our brain has about one hundred billion neurons. A neuron is the main character in the composition of the brain and reads the information transmitted from sensory organs such as the eyes, nose, or skin, transmitting it back to other neurons. Not only that, it has the ability to receive, send out, and process information—the most important tasks of the brain.

Not like the cells of other organs, the neuron of the brain has a distinctive feature in that the number of neurons, once set, is fixed. The number of cells in other parts of our body can be increased through cell division. The reason our wounds get healed is because the number of the cells of the wounded part increases. However, once a neuron gets damaged in an accident, the corresponding function suffers. And this is the reason why we have to pay careful attention and especially take care of the brain.

However, although the number of cells decreases, we can fortunately still expand the network that brings cells together even when we get old. This network is called synapse, and it connects between the neurons. Regardless of our age, the synapse keeps growing as long as stimulation is given. Whenever it grows, the brain regains its youth.

But if you are just satisfied with your familiar living style, you cannot give fresh stimulation to the brain, and this causes the degeneration of the brain. The decrease of the neurons caused by the aging process occurs mainly in the cerebrum and cerebellum—the centers of the intelligence function and motor control—and they degenerate easily. In other words, some disorders involving our intelligence function and motor functions will occur.

A BRAIN INSURANCE POLICY

Loss of cognitive function through dementia or Alzheimer's disease may be the most feared possible outcome of old age. Fortunately, walking has been shown to have high preventive value in this regard.

It has long been known that exercise can help protect the brain against the effects of aging. However, one study took it a step further. In that study, walking was shown to reverse brain shrinkage in a group of sixty- to eighty-year-olds. Their brains literally became bigger over the course of the study.

Additionally, a Swedish study found that people who exercised at least twice a week when they were younger had a much lower chance of developing Alzheimer's in old age. Walking, interestingly enough, was the most common form of exercise reported by the participants.

Walking is especially good for the brain because it involves a wide variety of brain functions working together simultaneously—balance and coordination come together in tandem with our five senses and our conscious mind. Essentially, walking is a kind of simultaneous cross training for the brain.

Consider the complex operations that are at work whenever you use the Jangsaeng Walking technique. All your senses must be engaged for total body awareness as you check body angles. Your arms swing freely on both sides of your body, engaging both sides of your brain. Your sense of balance is challenged and reinforced, and your conscious mind must work in tandem with your bodily movements. It is truly an ingenious process that we engage in every time we walk, and it is a great way to help maintain the brain.

Walking is a perfect exercise for BEST practitioners because it promotes bodily awareness and it offers endless opportunities to combine the complex motion of walking with use of the senses.

For the sake of the brain, I encourage you to keep your walks varied and to try to engage the senses fully as you walk. The most obvious way to do this is to vary your routes and to find unique places to walk. But more importantly, you should challenge your mind to discover new sights, sounds, and smells every time you walk, even if you are walking in a familiar place. It is easy for our brains to get in the rut of always noticing and thinking about the same things as we walk. So make a concerted effort to notice things you never noticed before and to engage your senses in new ways.

THE BREATHING BRAIN

Among the various operations that go on in the body, breathing is the one that affects the brain the most. It's because the brain must have oxygen in order to work. The brain takes up only two percent of the entire body; however it uses the most energy among the other parts of the body since it governs all human living activities, such as breathing, the heartbeat, exercising, and thoughts.

The brain consumes fifteen percent of the blood that pumps out of the heart, and even when it is resting without any activity, it consumes about twenty-five percent of the oxygen that comes in through breathing. Therefore in order to supply plenty of oxygen to the brain, one's blood circulation should be smooth. If the blood is not supplied to the brain for just fifteen seconds, the person will become unconscious, and in four minutes, the brain cells will be damaged to the point that they cannot be revived.

When you keep yawning or your head is foggy, it is because the brain cells are not activated. If this condition remains, your concentration level drops, you lack motivation, and your consciousness becomes dim.

Then how do we revive this tired brain? First of all, the brain should be supplied with plenty of oxygen. And in order to supply plenty of oxygen, one's blood circulation must be smooth. Most of us acknowledge that the heart should run smoothly in order to have smooth blood circulation, but we cannot operate the heart at will. However, we can move the feet at will. Therefore if we move and train the feet to help the operation of the heart, the whole body's blood circulation gets smoother and the supply of oxygen gets better, and now we can maintain a healthy condition from head to toe.

4. Doing the Leg Work

Your brain records habits easily. Every time you repeat a particular action, your brain uses the same set of circuitry, and those connections become all the more solidly reinforced. In essence, it is more comfortable for the brain to keep your same old habits, whether they are good for you or not.

REWIRE YOUR ROUTINE

It is no wonder it is so difficult to start and stick to a new exercise routine. Every time we make plans to change our patterns of behavior, the brain must create a whole new set of neural connections. This takes a lot of effort on the part of the brain! It can be exhausting, in fact. Our minds keep pulling us back to those old behaviors, even when we genuinely want to change.

Many New Year's resolutions are foiled every year because of this stubborn feature of the human brain.

You must be persistent about creating a good walking habit for yourself. When you first begin Jangsaeng Walking, you will undoubtedly feel a surge of energy as you move your body and align your energy system. But, as you proceed, you will also experience times of lower energy. This is the time when you are most vulnerable to falling back into old sedentary habits.

At these moments, make a special effort to continue with your fitness plan because these are the moments in which a new habit can be deliberately created. When you walk in the Jangsaeng style the first few times, there is no habit; the action is novel and naturally enjoyable. When you find yourself feeling tired and unmotivated to move well, recognize it as a natural part of the rewiring process. Your brain will want to fall back into the old routine, but you are the boss. You can say to your brain, "Sorry to inconvenience you, but I've decided we are going to do something else now."

When the brain builds a new set of connections to create a new habit, it is a little like building a new wing on your home. It is exhilarating when you first draw up the plans and start laying the foundation. But, at some point, the construction process is bound to be a little bit annoying—messy and exhausting. Maybe you even wish you had not started the project. Yet you carry on, knowing that eventually you will benefit from the addition to your home.

Stopping a fitness routine before it has become a habit is like abandoning a construction project in the middle. By following through with your fitness goals, you become like the foreman of your own brain, remodeling it toward the fit life you seek. When you hear a voice inside urging you to lay off for a while, make sure your brain knows who's the boss. Soon you will find that the fitness habit has become a simple, automatic part of your life.

A JOURNEY OF 10,000 STEPS

Both the U.S. surgeon general and the British Heart Association have suggested that people try to increase their walking to 10,000 steps a day in order to increase general fitness. For most people, that means doubling or tripling the amount they walk. You could measure your walking according to time or distance as well, but it is important to establish specific goals for yourself.

But don't try reaching the goal in one giant leap. If you want to go for the 10,000-step goal, first try counting the steps you take in an ordinary day. A pedometer is a relatively inexpensive tool that can help you do this. After you know how many steps you take in an average day, make a plan to add more steps, day by day.

Learn to welcome, rather than abhor, opportunities to use your legs more. For example, maybe you groan when you have to climb several flights of stairs. Perhaps you immediately look for the closest elevator. Really, you are just cheating yourself of an opportunity to energize yourself. Try applying the Jangsaeng Principles as you walk up the stairs, leaning forward on your Yong-chun, and you will feel the difference when you reach the top of the stairs.

We live in a convenience-obsessed society where we can take care of almost anything with just one phone call or mouse click. Although we are comfortable in the moment, our bodies' health and our brains' functions degenerate as we become more sedentary. If you want to avoid the many health problems that plague modern societies, start walking; walk as much as you can. You can prevent various symptoms that are caused by lack of exercise just by walking well.

FINDING THE TIME

In addition to the short walking snacks you add to your day, challenge yourself to take on extended bouts of walking. Try to find time for at least one one-hour walk per week, and take at least three walks of a half hour or longer each week. This will help you develop cardiovascular endurance, and it will help you take advantage of some of the more subtle benefits of walking, such as its stress-relieving qualities, which shorter walks may not permit.

You may ask, "When is the best time to walk?" The answer to that question depends on the benefits you are seeking. The morning is a wonderful time when the air is pure and fresh. Walking in the morning is a great way to start your day with a clear mind and to get in touch with yourself emotionally and spiritually.

On the other hand, the evening is also a wonderful time to walk and to reflect on the content of your day. Use an evening walk as a chance to release any emotions and tensions that have built up during the day. One study showed that people who walk after dinner are less likely to develop digestive problems like irritable bowel syndrome, so the evening may also be the best time to walk for physical health.

For beginners, I recommend trying different times during the day to see what works best for you. See how you feel mentally, physically, and emotionally with different walking schedules. Eventually, however, you should decide upon to a definite schedule for walking so it becomes an automatic part of your daily routine.

THE WALKING HABIT GESTATION

The body can only be healthy through good habits. Having expensive exercise equipment or taking various health supplements doesn't mean you will be healthy. The phrase "use it or lose it" applies to the body. The most important habit for health is to exercise regularly. The easiest and simplest way to do this is to increase the amount of steps we take in our daily life.

Never give in to your desire to get on the elevator right in front of you; use the stairs. When you see the elevator, think, "I'm not going to lose my exercise time!" to keep your resolution. And when you see the stairs, say, "Hey, nice to see you. You are the ultimate free gym!" Walk joyfully with the Jangsaeng method.

Do this regularly and your mind will change for the better, right along with your body.

Overview of Brain Education System Training

	Brain-oriented purpose	Commonly reported benefits	Recommended exercises for each step
step 1 **Sensitizing**	Awakening the brain-body senses	Physical health, enhanced focus and awareness	Stretching Energy awareness Breathing
step 2 **Versatilizing**	Making the brain more flexible and adaptable	Enhanced adaptability and creativity, more resilient mindset	Body balance Body-brain coordination Mental flexibility
step 3 **Refreshing**	Freeing one's brain from negative memories and habits	Positive outlook, self-confidence	Emotional release Partner healing Self-reflection
step 4 **Integrating**	Integrating brain functions and unleashing potential	Balanced, smoother behavior and activity	Circuit drawing Brain wave vibration Creativity exercises Energy-building exercises
step 5 **Mastering**	Enhanced executive control and faculty of imagination	Realizing the power of choice and creation, authorship of one's life	Meditation Brain screen Self-declaration

Brain Education
for Successful Aging Program

Brain Education (BE) for Successful Aging is a program that gives adults the tools they need to take an active role in generating and maintaining mental, physical, and emotional well-being. Using the latest findings in neuroscience and gerokinesiology, BE for Successful Aging draws upon exercises and activities that foster a sense of harmony between the brain and the body.

Based upon the five steps of Brain Education System Training (sensitizing, versatilizing, refreshing, integrating, and mastering), participants begin with a series of exercises that are designed to awaken the body and brain, to make the brain more flexible and adaptable, and to free it from negative emotional memories and habits. By progressing through each step, participants systematically learn how to integrate various brain functions, enhance executive control, and tap into their unlimited potential.

The goal of this program is to help participants realize that the power of the brain is not dependent upon age, but in the choices made in each moment. There is a tremendous level of power that exists within the brain that can be developed through the awareness of choice. This awareness allows one to gain true ownership of the brain, resulting in a more fulfilling life. Through Brain Education for Successful Aging, one is able to enjoy the benefits of a youthful mind and body along with the maturity and wisdom that comes with age and experience.

Benefits of the program include:

- Improved attention and concentration
- Better memory
- Expanded imagination and creativity
- More energy and stamina
- Mental sharpness
- Overall well-being and stress management

If you are considering BE for Successful Aging program for yourself or your community, please contact:

PowerBrain Education, LLC
450 Jordan Rd #2
Sedona, AZ 86336

info@powerbrainedu.com
www.powerbrainedu.com

The Senior Fitness Test

The Senior Fitness Test provides an easy and effective way to measure the strength, flexibility, and endurance of older adults without sophisticated equipment. Safe and enjoyable for older adults, it also meets scientific standards for reliability and validity. Developed by *In Full Bloom* coauthor Jessie Jones, Ph.D., and her colleague Roberta Rikli, Ph.D., its accompanying performance norms are based on actual performance scores of over seven thousand men and women between the ages of sixty and ninety-four. When completing the test, do the best you can, but do not overextend yourself or push yourself beyond what you consider safe. Prior to testing, complete a five- to ten-minute warm-up and general stretching routine.

This test was not developed specifically for use with the Brain Education System Training (BEST) method, but it is a great accompaniment. It is especially helpful for assessing progress during step one, which emphasizes the connection of body and brain. If you work with older adults, or if you would like to assess your own condition, try using this test before you begin. Usually it takes approximately three months of consistent practice to fully experience the benefits of BEST, so it is preferable to retest every three to six months.

30-SECOND CHAIR STAND

PURPOSE: Assesses lower-body strength, which is needed for numerous tasks, such as climbing stairs, walking, and getting out of a chair, tub, or car.

HOW TO TEST: Sit in a chair with your arms folded across your chest. Stand up, and then sit down again. Count the number of full stands you can complete in 30 seconds.

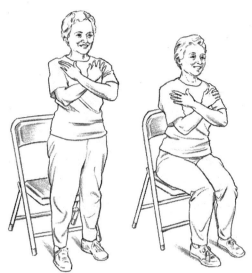

ARM CURL

PURPOSE: Tests upper-body strength, which is needed to perform household chores and other activities involving lifting and carrying items, such as groceries, suitcases, and grandchildren.

HOW TO TEST: Sit in a chair with one arm at your side, holding a hand weight—5 pounds (2.27 kilograms) for women and 8 pounds (3.63 kilograms) for men. Bend the elbow and bring the weight up to shoulder height, then extend the arm again to complete one biceps curl. Count the number of biceps curls that can be completed in 30 seconds.

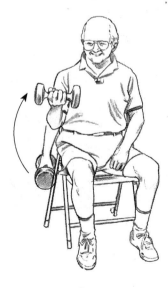

6-MINUTE WALK

PURPOSE: Measures aerobic endurance, which is important for walking long distances, climbing stairs, shopping, and sightseeing while on vacation.
HOW TO TEST: Record how many yards can be walked in 6 minutes around a 50-yard course. (5 yards = 4.57 meters.)

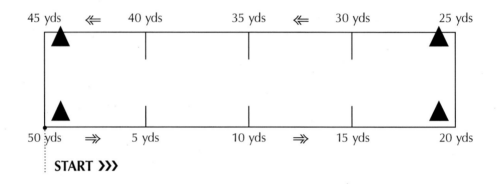

2-MINUTE STEP

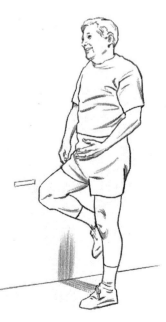

PURPOSE: Provides an alternate aerobic endurance test when space limitations or weather prohibit giving the 6-Minute Walk test.
HOW TO TEST: Stand up straight and raise one knee to a point midway between the patella (kneecap) and iliac crest (top of the hip bone). Lower your leg and repeat with the other knee. Continue steadily for 2 minutes and count the number of times the right knee reaches the required height.

CHAIR SIT-AND-REACH

PURPOSE: Assesses the lower body's flexibility, which is important for good posture, normal gait patterns, and for various mobility tasks, such as getting in and out of a bathtub or car.

HOW TO TEST: From a sitting position at the front of a chair, extend one leg out and reach toward your toes. Measure the approximate number of inches (1 inch = 2.5 centimeters) between the extended fingertips and the tip of the toe.

BACK SCRATCH

PURPOSE: Checks shoulder flexibility, which is important in everyday tasks such as combing hair, getting dressed, and reaching for a seat belt.

HOW TO TEST: With one hand reaching over the shoulder and behind the head and the other reaching behind the waist and up the middle of the back, measure the approximate number of inches (1 inch = 2.5 centimeters) between extended middle fingers.

8-FOOT UP-AND-GO

PURPOSE: Assesses agility and balance, which are important in daily tasks requiring quick maneuvering, such as getting off a bus or getting up to attend to something in the kitchen.

HOW TO TEST: Count the number of seconds required to get up from a seated position, walk 8 feet (2.44 meters), turn, and return to a seated position.

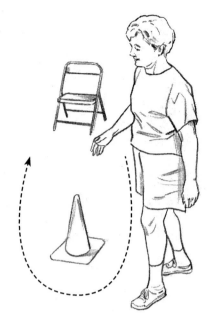

FUNCTIONAL FITNESS TEST FOR SENIORS

NORMAL RANGE OF SCORES

Age Group	60–64	65–69	70–74	75–79	80–84	85–89	90–94
Chair Stand (no. of stands)							
Women	12–17	11–16	10–15	10–15	9–14	8–13	4–11
Men	14–19	12–18	12–17	11–17	10–15	8–14	7–12
Arm Curl (no. of reps)							
Women	13–19	12–18	12–17	11–17	10–16	10–15	8–13
Men	16–22	15–21	14–21	13–19	13–19	11–17	10–14
6-Minute Walk (no. of yards walked)							
Women	545–660	500–635	480–615	430–585	385–540	340–510	275–440
Men	610–735	560–700	545–680	470–640	445–605	380–570	305–500
2-Minute Step (no. of steps)							
Women	75–107	73–107	68–101	68–100	60–91	55–85	44–72
Men	87–115	86–116	80–110	73–109	71–103	59–91	52–86
Chair Sit-and-Reach (inches)							
Women	-0.5–5.0	-0.5–4.5	-1.0–4.0	-1.5–3.5	-2.0–3.0	-2.5–2.5	-4.5–1.0
Men	-2.5–4.0	-3.0–3.0	-3.5–2.5	-4.0–2.0	-5.5–1.5	-5.5–0.5	-6.5–0.5
Back Scratch (inches)							
Women	-3.0–1.5	-3.5–1.5	-4.0–1.0	-5.0–0.5	-5.5–0.0	-7.0– -1.0	-8.0– -1.0
Men	-6.5–0.0	-7.5 – -1.0	-8.0– -1.0	-9.0– -2.0	-9.5– -2.0	-10.0– -3.0	-10.5– -4.0
8-ft Up-and-Go (seconds)							
Women	6.0–4.4	6.4–4.8	7.1–4.9	7.4–5.2	8.7–5.7	9.6–6.2	11.5–7.3
Men	5.6–3.8	5.7–4.3	6.0–4.2	7.2–4.6	7.6–5.2	8.9–5.3	10.0–6.2

Bibliography

American Society on Aging. "Marian Diamond's Optimism About the Aging Brain."
     Aging Today. May/June 1998.

Carmichael, Mary. "Stronger, Faster, Smarter." *Newsweek.* March 26, 2007.

Cohen, Gene D. T*he Creative Age: Awakening Human Potential in the Second Half of Life.*
     New York: Avon, 2000.

Cohen, Gene, M.D., Ph.D. "The Myth of the Mid Life Crisis." *Newsweek,*
     January 16, 2006.

Cohen, Gene D. *The Mature Mind: The Positive Power of the Aging Brain.* New York:
     Basic Books, 2007.

Crowley, Chris and Henry S. Lodge, M.D. *Younger Next Year: A Guide to Living Like You're 50
     Until You're 80 and Beyond.* New York: Workman, 2004.

Emory University Health Sciences Center. "Emory Study Lights Up The Political Brain."
     ScienceDaily. January 31, 2006.

Fukushima, Masanori, et al. "Evidence of Qi-gong Energy and its Biological Effect on
     the Enhancement of the Phagocytic Activity of Human Polymorphonuclear
     Leukocytes." *American Journal of Chinese Medicine.* 29.1. 2001. 1–16.

Goleman, Daniel. *Emotional Intelligence: Why It Can Matter More Than IQ.* New York:
     Bantam, 1997.

Hansen, Mark Victor; *Linkletter, Art. How to Make the Rest of Your Life the Best of Your Life.*
     Nashville: Nelson Books, 2006.

Ilchi, Lee. *Best 5 Handbook: Reaching Your Potential With Brain Education.* Sedona:
     Healing Society, 2007.

Ilchi, Lee. *Brain Respiration: Making Your Brain Creative, Peaceful and Productive.* Sedona:
     Healing Society, 2002.

Jones, Jessie C., and Debra J. Rose. *Physical Activity Instruction in Older Adults.*
     Champaign: Human Kinetics, 2005.

Kallejian, Verne, Ph.D., and Robert Griffeths, eds. "An Approach to Understanding Emotional Health (Part 3)." *www.healthandage.com,* August 16, 2006.

Kelly and Kelly et al. *Irreducible Mind: Toward a Psychology for the 21st Century.* Rowman and Littlefield, 2007.

Larson, Wang, Bowen, et al. "Exercise Is Associated with Reduced Risk for Incident Dementia among Persons 65 Years of Age and Older." *Annals of Internal Medicine.* 144.2 (2006).73–81.

Levy, Becca, Ph.D. and Michael Brickley, Ph.D. "Ohio Longitudinal Study of Aging and Retirement." *Journal of Personality and Social Psychology.* April 1, 2006.

Myers, David G. *The Pursuit of Happiness: Discovering the Path to Fulfillment, Well-Being and Enduring Personal Joy.* New York: Harper Paperbacks, 1993.

Penick, Jeffrey M. and Marte Fallshore. "Purpose and Meaning in Highly Active Seniors." *Adultspan Journal,* March 22, 2005.

Reynolds, Gretchen. "Lobes of Steel." *New York Times Play Magazine.* August 19, 2007.

Small, Gary. *The Memory Prescription: Dr. Gary Small's 14-Day Plan to Keep Your Brain and Body Young.* New York: Hyperion, 2004.

Somer, Elizabeth, M.A., R.D. *Age-Proof Your Body: Your Complete Guide to Looking and Feeling Younger.* New York: McGraw-Hill, 2006.

Taylor, S. E., et al. "Female Responses to Stress: Tend and Befriend, Not Fight or Flight." *Psychological Review.* 107(2003). 41–429.

Verghese, J. et al. "Leisure Activities and the Risk of Dementia in the Elderly." *New England Journal of Medicine.* 348(2003). 2508–16.

Wyoming Valley Health Care System Wellness Library. "Build a Buff Brain." *www.wvhc.staywellsolutionsonline.com.*

Yousheng, Shu, et al. "Modulation of Intracortical Synaptic Potentials by Presynaptic Somatic Membrane Potential." *Nature.* 441(2006). 761–765.

Index

A

abdominal organs, 64
abdominal tapping exercise, 58
abilities, latent, 137
absentmindedness, 108
acquired learning, 82
acquisition of wisdom, 83
active intellect, 77
adaptability, 14
adolescence, 110
AdultSpan Journal, 157
aerobic exercise, 40
affirmations, 164
age-itude inventory exercise, 118
aging
    and emotional processing, 109
    mental health and, 110
    myths about, 16–20
    positive attitude toward, 113
    rewards of, 20–21, 82–83
    roadblocks of, 132
    alignment, 180
alternate uses exercises, 97
alternating-finger count exercise, 88
Alzheimer's disease, 17, 75, 77–79, 200
    causes of, 78

dancing and, 81
American Journal of Chinese Medicine, 38–39
amino acids, 43
amygdala, 165
amyloid, 78
analog signals in brain, 130
arm fling exercise, 51
arthritis, 41
Asian medicine, 38
Asian spiritual traditions, 114
athletes, 76
attitudes, 41, 83, 113, 116, 157

B

balance, 90, 200
balance and mobility training, 41
BDNF (brain-derived neurotrophic factor), 19
beauty, 115
beliefs, 135
biases, 84, 108
biofeedback, 39
blessings, 115
blood pressure, 27, 42, 102
blood sugar levels, 42, 198

E

H

I

J

About the Authors

For the last three decades, Ilchi Lee has dedicated his life to finding ways to develop the potential of the human brain. Brain Education System Training (BEST), a collection of mind-body training programs that helps to unlock the brain's true potential, is the primary fruit of his search. The ultimate purpose of brain development, according to Lee, is lasting world peace. He identifies the brain as the seat of human consciousness, and therefore it is through developing the brain that he believes humanity may transcend its current condition.

Currently, Lee serves as the president of the University of Brain Education. Also, he is president of the Korea Institute of Brain Science and president of the International Brain Education Association. Lee is the author of thirty books, and his work as a peacemaker and educator has been widely recognized, both in his native Korea and in the international community.

For more information, visit www.ilchi.com.

Jessie Jones is a prolific scholar in the areas of gerontology, health, and exercise science. She currently serves as professor in the department of Health Science and as codirector of the Center for Successful Aging at California State University, Fullerton. She is a fellow for the American College of Sports Medicine and the American Academy for Kinesiology and Physical Education.

Jones is nationally and internationally known in the field of exercise science and aging for her research, program design, and curriculum development. Her work has been published in numerous professional journals and cited in over a hundred popular newspapers and magazines. She has conducted over on hundred professional presentations at conferences across the United Stated and around the world, including China, Taiwan, France, and Germany. She has led senior health and fitness programs for over twenty-five years, and has authored or co-authored several major books related to successful aging.

For more information, visit www.hdcs.fullerton.edu/csa.